EYEWITNESS

LIVING EARTH

EYEWITNESS

LIVING EARTH

Written and edited by
MIRANDA SMITH

A DORLING KINDERSLEY BOOK
London • New York • Munich • Melbourne • Delhi

DK

LONDON, NEW YORK, MUNICH,
MELBOURNE and DELHI

Senior editor Miranda Smith
Senior art editor Andrew Nash
Designer Joseph Hoyle
Senior managing editor Gillian Denton
Senior managing art editor Julia Harris
Production Catherine Semark
Editorial consultant Barbara Taylor

First published in Great Britain in 1996 by
Dorling Kindersley Limited,
80 Strand, London WC2R 0RL

Copyright © 1996
Dorling Kindersley Limited, London
This edition Published 2002
2 4 6 8 10 9 7 5 3 1
A CIP catalogue record for this book is
available from the British Library.

ISBN 0 7513 5388 4

Colour reproduction by
Colourscan, Singapore
Printed in Hong Kong/China by South
China Printing Co.

See our complete product line at
www.dk.com

CONTENTS

INTRODUCTION

THE EARTH IS HOME to millions of species, all with different characteristics and needs. How these species behave and interact with their environment and other species is a source of endless fascination. They survive in a variety of habitats and climates, from the frozen wastes of Antarctica to the tropical swamps of south-east Asia, from the teeming Australian barrier reef to the arid sands of the Namibian desert. The life-cycles of these animals and plants have been captured in superb detail by the photographers of the Eyewitness series, and provide a unique insight into the living earth.

FIRST FOSSILS

Fossils are the remains or impressions of living things that have hardened in rock. They tell scientists a great deal about the past, and the animals and plants that lived millions of years ago. The oldest fossils are 4,500 million years old and are of single-celled, bacteria-like organisms. It was another million years before an oxygen-rich atmosphere developed on earth, allowing more complex organisms to survive.

Fossil of rugose coral

Fossil of trilobite

Fossil of ammonite

FIRST STEPS

Four-legged animals took a major step forward when reptiles appeared. Unlike their amphibian ancestors, reptiles did not rely on an aquatic environment for survival. The land invasion from the swarming prehistoric seas that had been begun by plants, arthropods, and amphibians was complete. Today's lizards, such as this tegu lizard, *Tupinambus teguixin*, from tropical South America, are not very different in shape and characteristics from the prehistoric reptiles.

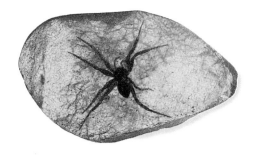

Spider preserved in amber

CHAPTER 1

FIRST LIFE

LIFE IS ONLY KNOWN here on earth, and earth's rocks contain fossils of past life that palaeontologists can use to construct the story of that life. The first fossils date from 4,500 million years ago, and from these early beginnings, very diverse forms of life developed, including reptiles, dinosaurs, and early mammals.

The sun

The sun viewed from earth, a violent storm erupting at its surface

THE SUN IS THE STAR at the centre of the solar system. It is 1.4 million kilometres (840,000 miles) in diameter and consists almost entirely of hydrogen and helium. The heat and light energy of the sun sustain life on earth. Without the sun, there would be no weather. Light from the sun is the energy which fuels the world's great weather machine, its heat keeping the atmosphere constantly in motion. Because the earth's surface is curved, the sun's rays strike different parts at different angles, dividing the world into distinct climate zones, each with its own typical weather.

Young stage of crab larva

Sample of zooplankton collected from north Atlantic coast of Scotland

Shrimp

LIFE IN THE SEA
Zooplankton are tiny, drifting animals that float in the oceans. They eat phytoplankton, minute, plants such as diatoms that need nutrients from the seawater and lots of sunlight to grow. Zooplankton in turn are eaten by larger fish, such as herring, which in their turn are eaten by still larger fish or other predators such as dolphins. Some larger ocean animals (whale sharks and blue whales) feed directly on zooplankton.

Shaving brush tree
Pachira aquatica

ANIMAL LIFE
All life on earth needs the sun to survive. Like all reptiles, a lizard is cold-blooded. This does not mean that its body is always cold, but that its temperature rises and falls with that of its surroundings. A lizard needs to be warm to move about, and it heats up its body by basking in the sunshine. If it gets too hot, it retreats into the shade. Insects also adjust their body in this way.

PLANT LIFE
The incredible variety of plant life on earth relies on its ability to convert the energy from sunlight into food (pp. 46–47), although only a tiny fraction of the sun's energy reaching the earth is actually used to create plant material. In shape and form, leaves are adapted to the task of capturing light; pigments such as chlorophyll and carotenoids absorb the light energy.

Energy emission
from the sun

Lower-energy
radiation

Sun

Earth

High-energy
radiation

FROM SUN TO EARTH

There are two kinds of energy that travel
from the sun to earth. High-energy
radiation (gamma rays) loses energy
while travelling to the surface of the sun
over a period of 2 million years. Lower-
energy radiation (mainly ultraviolet,
infrared, and light rays) travels to the
earth in only eight minutes.

Sun's core

HEAT AND LIGHT

In the sun's core, hydrogen is
converted to helium by nuclear fusion,
a process that releases energy. The
energy travels from the core to the
surface, where it leaves the sun in the
form of heat and light. The colour of a
star is determined by its temperature:
with the hottest stars blue and the
coolest red. The sun, with a surface
temperature of 5,500 °C (9,932°F), is
between these two extremes and
appears yellow in colour. Sometimes
huge loops of gas extend into the
solar atmosphere up to hundreds of
thousands of kilometres high. These
"prominences" can be seen from earth.

Prominence of
gas at the edge
of the sun's disc

Single-celled life

MOST FORMS OF LIFE consist of a single cell that carries out all the tasks involved in staying alive. With a few exceptions, single-celled organisms are so small that they cannot be seen with the naked eye, and until the 17th century no-one had any idea that they existed. The invention of the microscope revealed that single-celled creatures live almost everywhere, from pond water to household dust. Many exist on, and even in, the human body. During the 20th century, scientists have discovered that the many different forms of single-celled life fall into two distinct groups. Some cells have a nucleus and a range of special internal structures, organelles, that harness energy and put it to work. Other cells are smaller and simpler, with very few internal structures. These organisms – the bacteria – are the most abundant life form that exists. It is estimated that if all the bacteria in the world was weighed it would be 20 times more than the weight of all other living things put together.

EXPLORING A HIDDEN WORLD
The pioneering Dutchman Anton van Leeuwenhoek (1632–1723) designed and built this small single-lens microscope. In 1683, using this instrument, he became the first person to see bacteria. He made these sketches of the movements of bacteria that he found living on his teeth.

ANCIENT LIFE
These worm-like strands, photographed in ultraviolet light, are clusters of single-celled organisms called cyanobacteria. They make their food by using sunlight, and are the oldest living things to be found on the earth. Geologists have discovered huge fossilized mats of cyanobacteria, called stromatolites, that are over 3,000 million years old – almost three-quarters of the age of the planet itself.

MICROBES AND DISEASE
Research by the German bacteriologist Robert Koch (1843–1910) helped to prove that bacteria are one of the causes of disease. He found that certain bacteria grown from a culture in the laboratory could produce the deadly disease anthrax when introduced into cattle.

THE RACE TO REPRODUCE
A bacterium reproduces simply by dividing to make two new cells. Under ideal conditions, each bacterium can split into two every 20 minutes. Each of these two will then do the same, and so on. Within just a few hours, a single bacterium can produce a teeming colony of millions, like the one shown below.

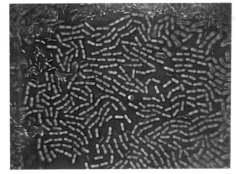

Fossilized plant-like organisms, known as diatoms

LIFE IN A SILICA CASE

The circle below is a collection of fossilized diatoms, tiny plant-like organisms that are far smaller than a pinhead and invisible to the naked eye. A diatom's single cell is supported by a beautifully sculpted case (right) made of silica, a material found in sand and similar to glass. The case consists of two halves that fit over each other, and each species has a case of a slightly different shape. In the 19th century, the arranging of diatoms became a craze. One microscopist managed to squeeze all the diatoms then known – over 4,000 species – into a square less than 7 mm (0.3 in) across.

Silica skeleton

Scanning electron micrograph of boat-shaped diatom

Light microscope image of amoeba

Pseudopod

PLANT ADRIFT

Desmids are plant-like organisms found in water that is poor in nutrients. A desmid's single cell has a narrow "waist", making it look like two cells that are joined together. The green colour in this light microscope image is produced by the presence of the green colouring matter chlorophyll in the cell.

CHANGING SHAPE

Unlike diatoms and desmids, an amoeba is a microscopic predator. Its single cell has no fixed shape, and it moves by putting out "false feet", pseudopods, into which the body of the cell flows. The amoeba feeds by surrounding other organisms and engulfing them.

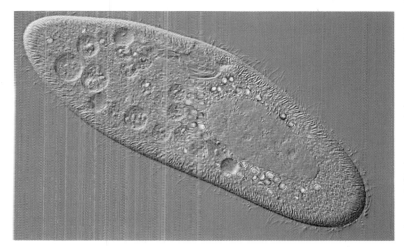

HIGH-SPEED SLIPPER

This *Paramecium*, once called a "slipper animalcule", is one of the fastest movers in the single-celled world. It is covered with thousands of tiny hairs, or cilia, that act like microscopic oars to push it through the water. It moves so quickly that light microscopists have to add a thickening agent to the water to slow it down sufficiently to study it.

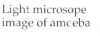

PRESERVED IN STONE

The masons and workers of ancient Egypt built the pyramids using a kind of rock called nummulitic limestone. It is made entirely from the cases of single-celled marine organisms called foraminiferans. The rock forms when countless trillions of these microscopic skeletons build up into a thick layer on the bed of an ancient sea, and the remains are slowly compressed.

Carbon on the move

ALL LIVING THINGS contain the element carbon. It is
also found in the oceans, in the air, and in the earth
itself. Carbon combines with other substances to
take on different forms. In the atmosphere, with
oxygen, it exists as carbon dioxide (CO_2). In the
ground, and in the bones and shells of animals,
carbon is found in the form of chalky calcium
carbonate. Carbon is passed around the
biosphere, with plants as the main point
of exchange. They convert the
atmospheric CO_2 into carbohydrates,
a source of energy used to maintain
their everyday processes, through
photosynthesis (pp. 40–41). When
living things die, they are broken
down by bacteria known as
decomposers. The carbon that
they needed to live is released
back into the atmosphere to
be used by other forms of life.

STORES OF CARBON
As plants grow, they absorb carbon from
the atmosphere. Some of this carbon is
used immediately by the plant, but
some is stored by being incorporated
into their structure, for example as
starch (p. 40). Every tree trunk is
a store of carbon. When the
tree is burnt, this carbon is
released back into the
atmosphere as
carbon dioxide.

THE CARBON CYCLE

Less than one per cent of carbon on Earth is in active circulation in the biosphere. The rest is locked up as inorganic carbon in rocks, and as organic carbon in fossil fuels. Growing plants take in carbon dioxide from the atmosphere and incorporate this in their structure as carbohydrate. In this form carbon passes into the food chains. The plants release stored energy by a process called respiration in which plants break down the carbohydrates. This releases energy and produces carbon dioxide as a waste product.

CO_2 removed from air during photosynthesis

CO_2 released into the air during respiration of tree

Droppings and remains from carnivorous animals

CO_2 released by breathing animals

Droppings and remains from herbivorous animals

Falling leaves and branches

CO_2 released from droppings and remains by decomposition

CO_2 released from leaf-litter by fungi and invertebrates

Ecosystems circulate carbon at different rates. In a tropical rainforest where plants grow quickly, the rate is 100 times greater than in a desert.

SECONDHAND ENERGY

Animals depend on plants to obtain carbon. They may feed on plants directly or eat animals that have fed on plants. The nut that this chipmunk is consuming is carbohydrate which the tree has converted from carbon dioxide by photosynthesis and stored. All animals are living stores of carbon. However, they release some of this as carbon dioxide in the breath that they exhale.

FEEDING THE YOUNG

When the adults of some salmon species have migrated upriver and spawned, they are so exhausted that they die. Their bodies lie rotting in great numbers in the river's headwaters. This provides a supply of nutrients for the eggs to grow and also for the young salmon when they hatch. The young are effectively made up of carbon from their parents.

CARBON AS A FOSSIL FUEL

Carbon is locked in the remains of living things that fail to decompose completely. During the Carboniferous period, 363–290 million years ago, plants died in the shallow swamps, forming thick layers. Over millions of years, the heat of the earth and the pressure of material building up on top of them turned this carbon into coal. In a similar way, vast deposits of tiny dead sea creatures became a liquid store of carbon – oil, which can be converted into petrol. When these "fossil fuels" are burned, the carbon is finally released. Carbon locked up in the earth's coal and oil is estimated as 50 times as much as there is in all living things. However, reserves of coal will only last about 250–300 years if it is used at the current rate, while oil will probably only last 100 years.

The surface of the earth

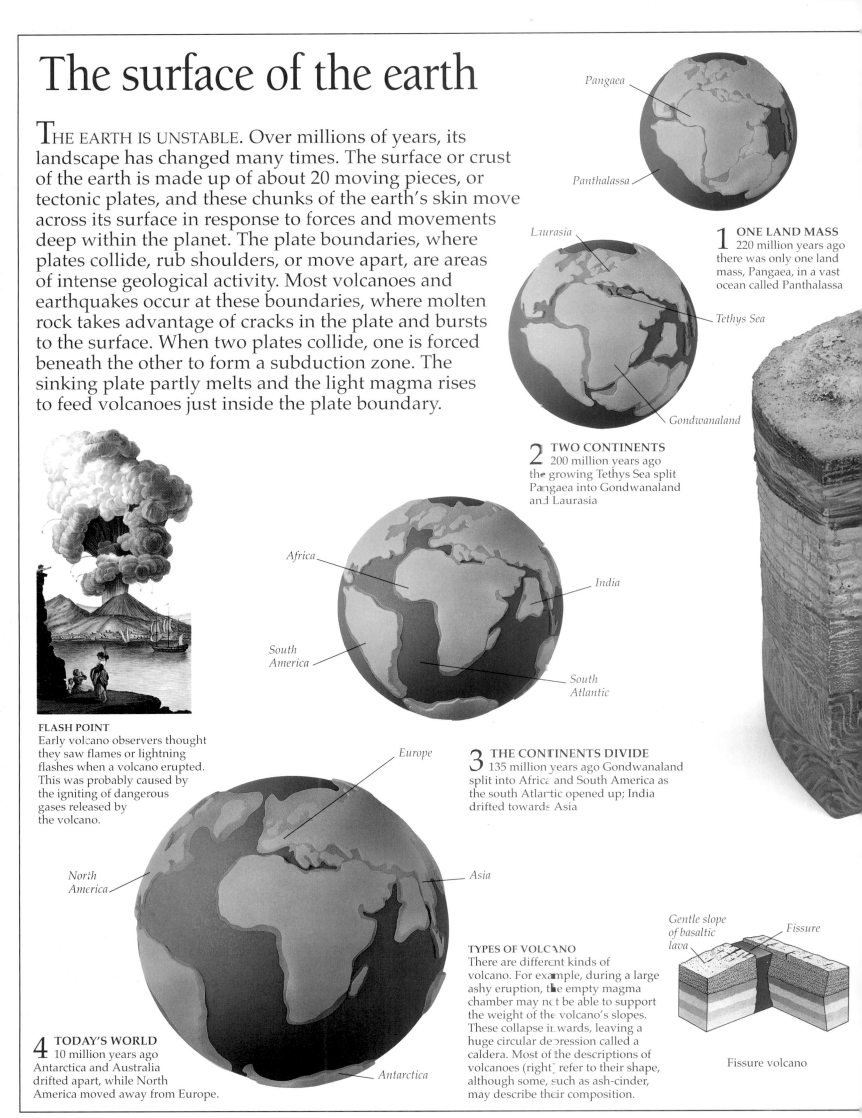

THE EARTH IS UNSTABLE. Over millions of years, its landscape has changed many times. The surface or crust of the earth is made up of about 20 moving pieces, or tectonic plates, and these chunks of the earth's skin move across its surface in response to forces and movements deep within the planet. The plate boundaries, where plates collide, rub shoulders, or move apart, are areas of intense geological activity. Most volcanoes and earthquakes occur at these boundaries, where molten rock takes advantage of cracks in the plate and bursts to the surface. When two plates collide, one is forced beneath the other to form a subduction zone. The sinking plate partly melts and the light magma rises to feed volcanoes just inside the plate boundary.

Pangaea

Panthalassa

1 ONE LAND MASS
220 million years ago there was only one land mass, Pangaea, in a vast ocean called Panthalassa

Laurasia

Tethys Sea

Gondwanaland

2 TWO CONTINENTS
200 million years ago the growing Tethys Sea split Pangaea into Gondwanaland and Laurasia

FLASH POINT
Early volcano observers thought they saw flames or lightning flashes when a volcano erupted. This was probably caused by the igniting of dangerous gases released by the volcano.

Africa

India

South America

South Atlantic

3 THE CONTINENTS DIVIDE
135 million years ago Gondwanaland split into Africa and South America as the south Atlantic opened up; India drifted towards Asia

Europe

Asia

North America

4 TODAY'S WORLD
10 million years ago Antarctica and Australia drifted apart, while North America moved away from Europe.

Antarctica

TYPES OF VOLCANO
There are different kinds of volcano. For example, during a large ashy eruption, the empty magma chamber may not be able to support the weight of the volcano's slopes. These collapse inwards, leaving a huge circular depression called a caldera. Most of the descriptions of volcanoes (right) refer to their shape, although some, such as ash-cinder, may describe their composition.

Gentle slope of basaltic lava

Fissure

Fissure volcano

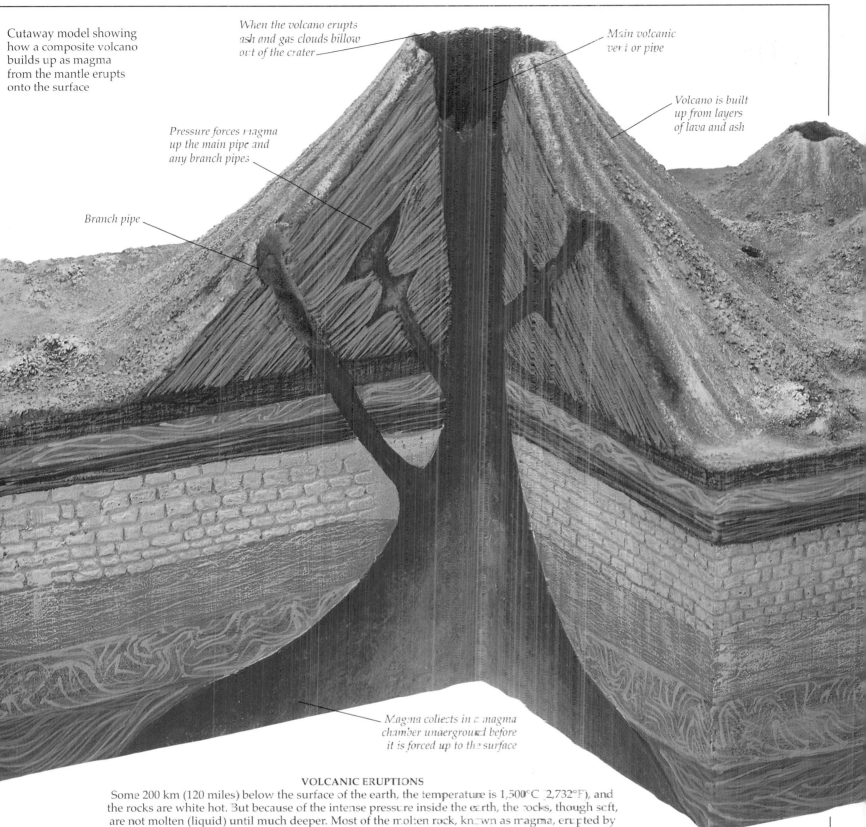

Cutaway model showing how a composite volcano builds up as magma from the mantle erupts onto the surface

When the volcano erupts ash and gas clouds billow out of the crater

Main volcanic vent or pipe

Volcano is built up from layers of lava and ash

Pressure forces magma up the main pipe and any branch pipes

Branch pipe

Magma collects in a magma chamber underground before it is forced up to the surface

VOLCANIC ERUPTIONS

Some 200 km (120 miles) below the surface of the earth, the temperature is 1,500°C (2,732°F), and the rocks are white hot. But because of the intense pressure inside the earth, the rocks, though soft, are not molten (liquid) until much deeper. Most of the molten rock, known as magma, erupted by volcanoes comes from the top of the mantle, 100 to 300 km (60 to 180 miles) down. Because magma is hotter and lighter than the surrounding rocks, it rises, melting some of the rocks it passes on the way. If it manages to find a way to the surface, the magma will erupt as lava.

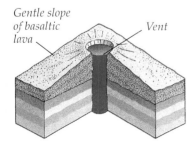

Gentle slope of basaltic lava

Vent

Shield volcano

Steep, convex slope

Vent

Dome volcano

Fine ash

Cinder

Ash-cinder volcano

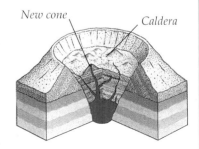

New cone

Caldera

Caldera volcano

The changing earth

FOR ALMOST 1,000 MILLION YEARS, nothing lived on earth. Nothing wriggled or ran, flew or swam. That ancient, lifeless earth was very different from the world today. But as the early planet was constantly changing – as new rocks were formed, mountains were created, oceans gradually spread, earthquakes and volcanoes shook and rattled the surface, continents slowly shifted, and climates changed – the chance was created for life to exist. Today, evidence of that life is preserved as fossils found on the earth's rocky surface.

HOT ROCKS
Volcanoes occur at weak, thin points in the earth's crust. Molten lava is poured out of fissures and solidifies as it cools. Ash and hot gases are thrown into the air and the ash falls to form a volcanic cone. In the early stages of the earth's formation, the world was a hot mass of molten rock.

Sandstone is made of eroded grains of quartz

Metamorphic marble was sedimentary limestone

Granite solidified deep underground

Basalt is a common volcanic igneous rock

BUILDING BLOCKS
Igneous rocks form from molten rock material deep in the earth and at the surface. Rock particles eroded by wind and water form sedimentary layers in rivers, seas, and lakes. Changes in temperature and pressure can transform both igneous and sedimentary rocks into metamorphic rocks.

WATERY GRAVES
Rivers build thick sedimentary layers of sand and mud on flood plains and deltas. Reaching the sea, the sediment sinks to the sea floor. Animal and plant remains may be preserved as the sediments turn to rock.

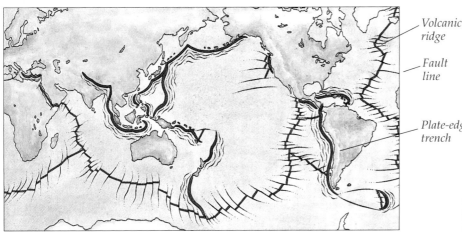

Volcanic ridge

Fault line

Plate-edge trench

The "part" of a trilobite

MOVING PLATES
The earth's surface is made of interlocking plates separated by fractures and faults. Spreading out from volcanic ridges on the ocean floor, plate edges may sink in deep trenches where earthquakes and volcanoes can occur. Less dense land masses, the continents, are carried on these plates, and collisions can produce huge mountain ranges, such as the Himalayas in Asia.

FOSSIL EVIDENCE
Splitting apart a fossil rock reveals the positive "part" (above) of the fossil and the negative "counterpart" (right), the natural mould. Fossils are evidence of ancient animal and plant life. They may preserve an organism's detailed inner structure as well as its outer shape. Flowers, feathers, and even footprints can be fossilized. The conversion of buried organisms into stony replicas takes millions of years, as the organic material is destroyed and minerals in the rocks slowly fill microscopic shapes. Sometimes the buried fossil is destroyed completely in the rock, leaving a natural mould.

How a fossil is formed

A decaying *Procolophon* (1) was covered in silt sediment swept in by shallow streams (2). Burial must have been rapid since the skeleton was not broken up, although the flesh rotted. Over millions of years, the skeleton was buried deep underground (3). Under pressure, sands became stone, in which chemicals turned the bones into fossil. Erosion brought the fossil back to the surface (4).

1. Decaying and dead *Procolophon* carcass lies exposed on Earth's surface

2. Silt sediments from shallow streams quickly bury the reptile's body

3. Sediments turn to rock around the fossil over millions of years

4. Fossilized skeleton is exposed at the surface

"Counterpart" of a trilobite, *Flexicalymene caractaci*

Procolophon trigoniceps
South Africa

SMALL REPTILE

Procolophon was a small reptile which lived 245 million years ago. Its fossils from the Karroo Basin in South Africa are well known. Complete skeletons and skulls, perfectly preserved as white fossil bone, are buried in a red silty rock. This red colour comes from iron minerals which hold the quartz grains together. The colour indicates that the sediment was exposed to air and not continuously buried underwater.

HOT AND COLD

Rocks preserve clues about prehistoric climatic conditions which help to explain the shifting continents. Fossils of the large-leaved *Glossopteris* are found in abundance in Antarctic Permian rocks. During this period, the Antarctic, part of a much larger continental mass, was not at the South Pole. Its climate was much warmer than today.

Fossil leaf

Glossopteris, Permian, New South Wales, Australia

MOULDED FROM LIFE

The natural mould left by a buried fossil fills with rock material, and produces an accurate cast of the fossil's shape. This trilobite's overall shape has been preserved, but the hard fossil skeleton was destroyed over many years. Fossils are often flattened under the pressure of rock above and may be cracked and broken into many pieces.

OLD AGE

Evidence from meteorites and moon rocks show that the earth is 4,550 million years old. The oldest rocks on earth, about 3,750 million years old, are found in Greenland and are metamorphic. Originally sediments, some of these rocks were laid down at an even earlier stage.

Turning to stone

THE PROCESS OF CHANGING from a living organism to a fossil takes place over millions of years. Fossilization is a very chancy process. As soon as animals and plants die, they begin to decompose, or rot. The hard parts, such as the shells, bones, and teeth of animals, or the wood of plants, last longer than soft tissue but they are often scattered by animals, wind, or flowing water. In order for something to be fossilized it must be buried quickly before it decomposes. This is most likely to be done by sediment, like sand or mud, washed over the fossil by water. Some fossils later dissolve; others may be changed chemically or distorted due to high temperatures and pressures. Only a tiny fraction will survive to be found.

LAND SHAPES
Over millions of years, rocks are eroded and shaped by wind and water, bringing ancient fossils to the surface.

2 DECAYING MUSSEL
When the mussel dies, the two chalky shells open out into a "butterfly" position. The soft parts of the mussel enclosed by the shells soon begin to rot or are eaten by scavenging animals.

Living mussel

Living mussels attach themselves to rocks by byssal threads

1 LIVING MUSSEL
The soft parts of the mussel are enclosed by two chalky shells. Each individual may spend its entire life in one place, and dense masses form mussel beds. If a mussel becomes detached it may die, especially if it is swept into a different environment.

PRESERVATION TO DISCOVERY

These four drawings show how animals and plants can be preserved and their remains discovered millions of years later. It is a very slow process and the climate and shape of the land will probably change as much as the animal and plant life.

1. Dead animals sink to the seabed and their remains are buried by layers of sediment.

2. The lower layers of sediment turn to rock and the remains harden to form fossils.

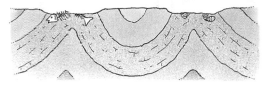

3. The rock is gradually folded and eroded

4. The fossils are exposed on the surface.

Soft parts have rotted away

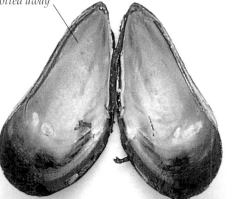

3 **HARD PARTS REMAIN**
When the soft parts of shells such as the mussel have rotted away, the hard parts, in other words the shells, remain.

4 **TOWARDS FOSSILIZATION**
The shells of dead mussels are often carried along by currents in the water and dropped together in one area where they are mixed with pebbles and sand to form "mussel beaches". Some of the individuals shown here still have their two shells held together by a tough bit of tissue called a ligament. Constant battering by the sea may break some shells into very small pieces. All these may then be buried and eventually they become fossilized.

Separated shell

Tough ligament holding shells together

Fossil mussel shell!

5 **FOSSILIZED MUSSELS**
Many small mussels become firmly embedded in rock. Here, a natural mineral-cement binds the sediment grains and fossil shells together, making it difficult for a collector to take the shells out.

FOSSILS WITH COLOUR
The shells of living mussels are deep blue. Some of the blue colour is still visible in these fossil mussels, which are an incredible two million years old.

LOST COLOUR
The colour in shells is usually lost during the process of fossilization. The brown colour in these fossils is from the rock in which they were fossilized.

Life in the ancient seas

THE EARTH, WITH ITS VAST EXPANSES of ocean, has not always looked the way it does today. Over millions of years the land masses have drifted across the face of the earth as new oceans have opened up and old oceans disappeared. Today's oceans only started to take shape in the last 200 million years of the earth's 4,500-million-year existence. Simple organisms first appeared in the oceans 3,300 million years ago and were followed by more and more complex life forms. As the oceans changed, so too did life in the waters. Soft-bodied creatures evolved into animals with hard shells, and trilobites flexed their external skeletons with internal muscles, alongside gigantic marine reptiles, such as the plesiosaurs. Some forms of life eventually became extinct, while others still survive in the oceans today, and are more or less unchanged.

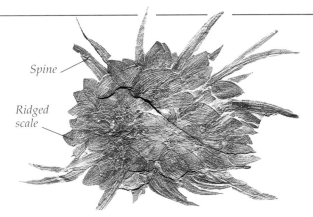

Spine

Ridged scale

TOPSY-TURVY WORLD
Wiwaxia lived on the sea floor 530 million years ago, yet this fossil was found high above sea level in Canada's Rocky Mountains. This shows just how much the earth's surface has changed, and how land, originally formed under the sea, was forced up to form mountain chains.

Strong belly ribs protected the underside of the bulky, rounded body

Short tail relative to total body length

Pelvic girdle

Femur, or thigh bone

Huge, long, flat flipper made up of five rows of elongated toes

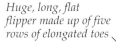

Arm used for moving and catching food

Fossil brittle star, *Palaeocoma*

STILL HERE TODAY
This 180-million-year-old fossil brittle star looks like its living relative (above). Brittle stars have a round central disc and five very fragile, jointed arms, that can easily break. Today, as in the past, large numbers are often found on sandy or muddy seabeds.

ANCIENT CORAL

Compared to their soft-bodied relatives the anemones and jellyfish, corals such as this 400-million-year-old fossil have been preserved well in rocks because of their hard skeletons. Each coral animal formed a skeleton that joined that of its neighbour to create a network of chains with large spaces between them.

CHANGING OCEANS

One giant ocean, Panthalassa, surrounded the super-continent Pangaea (290–240) mya (million years ago). At the end of this period, many kinds of marine life became extinct. Pangaea broke up, with part drifting north and part south, with the Tethys Sea between.

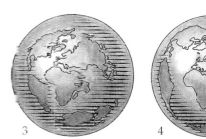

CONTINENTAL DRIFT

The northern part split to form the North Atlantic 208–146 mya (2). The South Atlantic and Indian Oceans began to form 146–65 mya (3). The continents continued to drift 1.64 mya (4). Today the oceans are still changing shape – the Atlantic Ocean gets wider by a few centimetres each year.

Most flexible vertebrae in neck

Long neck and small head typical of one type of plesiosaur

Plated arm in life had feather-like feeding structures

Sharp, interlocking teeth for capturing fish prey

MARINE REPTILES

The first reptiles mostly lived on land, but some of their spectacular descendants became adapted for life in the sea. Among the best known are the plesiosaurs that first appeared around 200 million years ago. Plesiosaurs swam using their flippers – as either oars or wings – to "fly" through the water like marine turtles do today. They eventually died out around 65 million years ago at the same time as their land-based cousins, the dinosaurs. The only true ocean-dwelling reptiles today are the sea snakes and sea turtles.

All-round vision provided by large, curved eye

Smaller front flipper also had five elongated toes

SEA LILY

A complete fossil of a sea lily (crinoid) is quite a rare find even though large numbers of these animals grew on the bottom of ancient oceans. The skeleton, composed of small bony plates, usually broke up when the animal died. Although they are far less numerous today, sea lilies are still found living below 100 m (330 ft). Sea lilies are relatives of feather stars, but unlike them are usually anchored firmly to the seabed. Their arms surround an upward-facing mouth and are used to trap small particles of food that drift by.

Segmented body allowed trilobite to roll up like a woodlouse

Long, flexible stem anchored crinoid in seabed gardens

DEAD AND GONE

Trilobites, one of the most abundant creatures living in the ancient seas, first flourished over 510 million years ago. They had jointed limbs as well as an external skeleton like insects and crustaceans (such as crabs and lobsters). Trilobites died out some 250 million years ago.

Fossil evidence

ABOUT 470 MILLION YEARS AGO, one group of animals – the vertebrates – escaped the restrictions of living in shells. They developed an internal, bony skeleton, and this anchored muscles and supported internal organs. Bones, teeth, and scales are tough and preserve well, so there is plenty of fossil evidence. The first vertebrates were jawless fishes, and some of them, such as cephalaspids and placoderms, carried a heavy outer armour. Many were restricted to living on seabeds. Later fish had less of a bony covering on their heads, and developed toothed, gaping jaws. The success of advanced bony fishes, the teleosts, is seen in the vast numbers of these mobile fishes living today in rivers, lakes, and seas.

Spiny pectoral fin for punting along muddy sea floor

Fossil of Pterichthyodes milleri

HEAVY ARMOUR
One of the most armoured of the placoderm fish – the 370-million-year-old, 13-cm (5-in) long *Pterichthyodes* – had no inner bone skeleton. Instead, it had a hard shell of bony plates that covered both the head and body. Even the fish's pectoral fins were enclosed in a bony casing and would not have been much use for swimming.

Large eye

Fossil of Cephalaspis pagei

SENSITIVE SUCKER
The first fish were jawless, sucking food and water through their mouths. *Cephalaspis* had a bony shield covering its jawless head, as well as a pair of pectoral fins protected by swept-back spines. Two eyes and a single nostril perched on the crest of the arched head shield, which had three sensitive, scale-covered patches connected to the brain. *Cephalaspis* was an ostracoderm – it had a "bony skin".

Symmetrical two-part tail fin

Fossil of Lepidotes elvensis

Modern African lungfish

Dorsal fin supported on ray of fine bones

Armoured head

Remains of concretion

EXPOSED WITH ACID
Unlike modern lungfishes, which live in freshwater, the prehistoric lungfish *Chirodipterus* lived in shallow seas. It was covered in thick, bony scales and had an armoured head. This specimen from Australia was preserved in a hard chalky concretion. The fossil was exposed by being bathed in acid, which dissolved some of the concretion but not the fish inside.

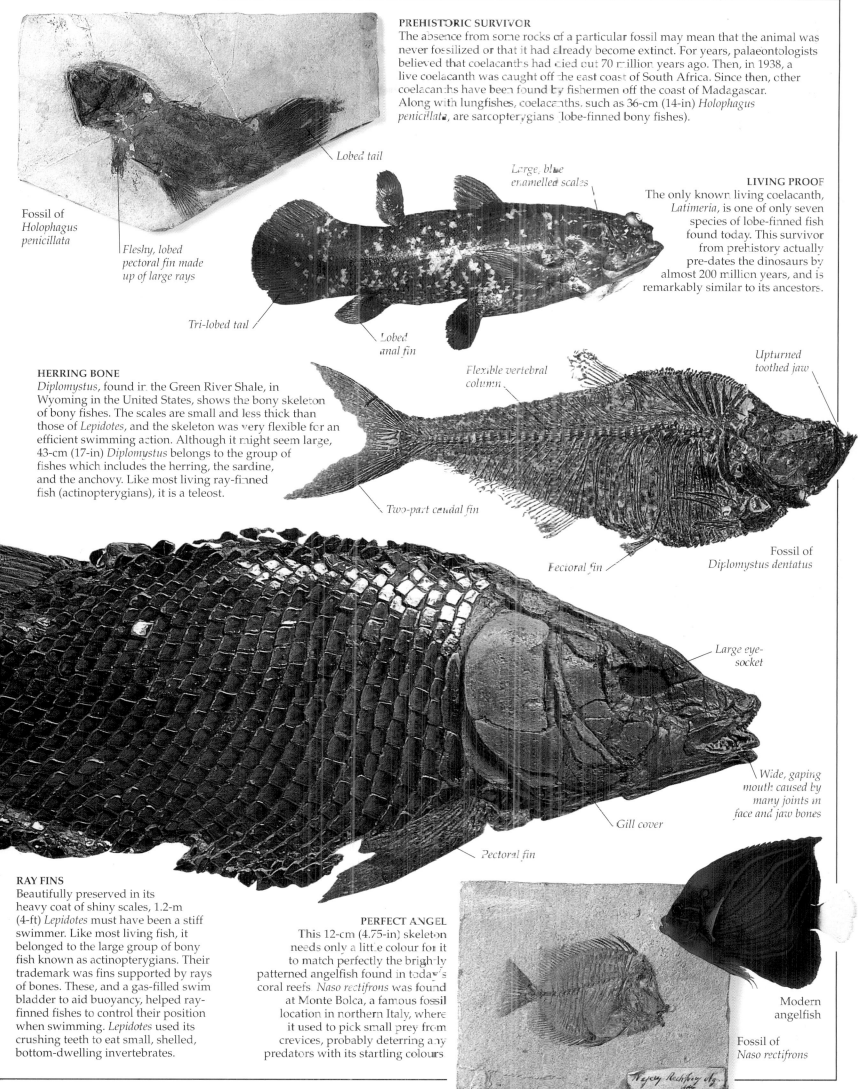

PREHISTORIC SURVIVOR

The absence from some rocks of a particular fossil may mean that the animal was never fossilized or that it had already become extinct. For years, palaeontologists believed that coelacanths had died out 70 million years ago. Then, in 1938, a live coelacanth was caught off the east coast of South Africa. Since then, other coelacanths have been found by fishermen off the coast of Madagascar. Along with lungfishes, coelacanths. such as 36-cm (14-in) *Holophagus penicillata*, are sarcopterygians (lobe-finned bony fishes).

Lobed tail

Fossil of *Holophagus penicillata*

Fleshy, lobed pectoral fin made up of large rays

Large, blue enamelled scales

Tri-lobed tail

Lobed anal fin

LIVING PROOF

The only known living coelacanth, *Latimeria*, is one of only seven species of lobe-finned fish found today. This survivor from prehistory actually pre-dates the dinosaurs by almost 200 million years, and is remarkably similar to its ancestors.

HERRING BONE

Diplomystus, found in the Green River Shale, in Wyoming in the United States, shows the bony skeleton of bony fishes. The scales are small and less thick than those of *Lepidotes*, and the skeleton was very flexible for an efficient swimming action. Although it might seem large, 43-cm (17-in) *Diplomystus* belongs to the group of fishes which includes the herring, the sardine, and the anchovy. Like most living ray-finned fish (actinopterygians), it is a teleost.

Flexible vertebral column

Upturned toothed jaw

Two-part caudal fin

Pectoral fin

Fossil of *Diplomystus dentatus*

Large eye-socket

Wide, gaping mouth caused by many joints in face and jaw bones

Gill cover

Pectoral fin

RAY FINS

Beautifully preserved in its heavy coat of shiny scales, 1.2-m (4-ft) *Lepidotes* must have been a stiff swimmer. Like most living fish, it belonged to the large group of bony fish known as actinopterygians. Their trademark was fins supported by rays of bones. These, and a gas-filled swim bladder to aid buoyancy, helped ray-finned fishes to control their position when swimming. *Lepidotes* used its crushing teeth to eat small, shelled, bottom-dwelling invertebrates.

PERFECT ANGEL

This 12-cm (4.75-in) skeleton needs only a little colour for it to match perfectly the brightly patterned angelfish found in today's coral reefs. *Naso rectifrons* was found at Monte Bolca, a famous fossil location in northern Italy, where it used to pick small prey from crevices, probably deterring any predators with its startling colours.

Modern angelfish

Fossil of *Naso rectifrons*

Reptiles reign

THE FIRST REPTILES appeared 360–290 million years ago and probably did not look very different from their amphibian ancestors. For 200 million years, they colonized the continents, and dominated the earth. Many reptiles evolved on land, including the dinosaurs, while others such as the pterosaurs took to the air, and some, such as the mesosaurs, lived in the sea. Many reptiles were amniotes: they produced an egg which enclosed the developing embryo in its own wet world, protecting it with a tough, waterproof shell. Reptiles were the first amniotes, followed by birds and mammals.

HOT STUFF
Reptiles were many different shapes. *Dimetrodon*, a meat-eating pelycosaur, was 3 m (10 ft) long, and carried a huge fan of skin along its back which acted as a giant radiator and heat absorber.

Dry, scaly skin

SETTING SAIL
The plant-eating *Edaphosaurus* had a skin sail supported on long, vertebral spines with cross pieces. It was a pelycosaur – a lizard with a basin-shaped pelvis.

Flattened skull

Pelvis, legs, and five-toed feet separated from body

Backbone with ribs attached

REPTILE FIRST
From a small quarry in central Scotland, this distorted 20-cm (8-in) long fossil skeleton (nicknamed "Lizzie") is one of the most important fossils ever found. Sandwiched between fine rock layers, 338-million-year-old *Westlothiana lizziae* is the oldest reptile and amniote to have been found.

Very long body

Model of *Westlothiana lizziae* (viewed from above), based on scientific research and artist's impression

Individual spine in backbone

UNDERSTANDING THE EVIDENCE
Westlothiana was discovered in ancient rocks formed in a lake fed by hot, volcanic spring water. Four-legged, as well as legless, snake-like amphibian skeletons were also found, along with spiders, scorpions, and millipedes. Tree-sized seed ferns grew nearby. *Westlothiana* was about 30 cm (1 ft) long, its long body balanced on short legs. Some, but not all, features of the skull and limb bones match those found in later reptiles. It is not surprising that *Westlothiana*, so like its amphibian ancestors, is not easily distinguished from them.

Tail made up a large part of whole body length

Scales on skin helped keep Westlothiana waterproof

Long, lizard-like tail

Neural spine of backbone helped form skin-covered sail of *Edaphosaurus*

Model of first known reptile, *Westlothiana lizziae*

Mottled scales for camouflage

Each foot had five toes

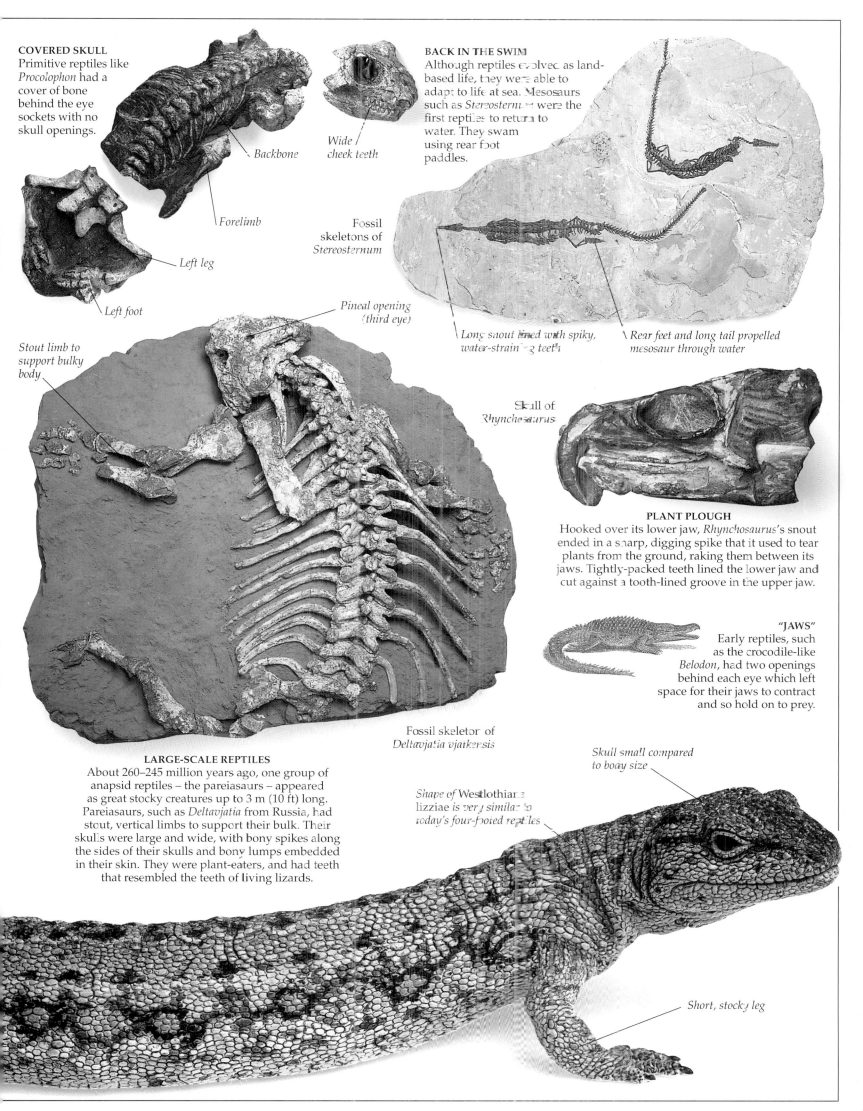

COVERED SKULL
Primitive reptiles like *Procolophon* had a cover of bone behind the eye sockets with no skull openings.

Backbone

Forelimb

Left leg

Left foot

Wide cheek teeth

Stout limb to support bulky body

Pineal opening (third eye)

BACK IN THE SWIM
Although reptiles evolved as land-based life, they were able to adapt to life at sea. Mesosaurs such as *Stereosternum* were the first reptiles to return to water. They swam using rear foot paddles.

Fossil skeletons of *Stereosternum*

Long snout lined with spiky, water-straining teeth

Rear feet and long tail propelled mesosaur through water

Skull of *Rhynchosaurus*

PLANT PLOUGH
Hooked over its lower jaw, *Rhynchosaurus*'s snout ended in a sharp, digging spike that it used to tear plants from the ground, raking them between its jaws. Tightly-packed teeth lined the lower jaw and cut against a tooth-lined groove in the upper jaw.

"JAWS"
Early reptiles, such as the crocodile-like *Belodon*, had two openings behind each eye which left space for their jaws to contract and so hold on to prey.

Fossil skeleton of *Deltavjatia vjatkensis*

LARGE-SCALE REPTILES
About 260–245 million years ago, one group of anapsid reptiles – the pareiasaurs – appeared as great stocky creatures up to 3 m (10 ft) long. Pareiasaurs, such as *Deltavjatia* from Russia, had stout, vertical limbs to support their bulk. Their skulls were large and wide, with bony spikes along the sides of their skulls and bony lumps embedded in their skin. They were plant-eaters, and had teeth that resembled the teeth of living lizards.

Shape of Westlothiana lizziae is very similar to today's four-footed reptiles

Skull small compared to body size

Short, stocky leg

29

Birth of the dinosaurs

Gᴵᴬⁿᵀ PREDATORS, lumbering plant processors, agile browsers, and pack hunters – dinosaurs occupy an impressive place in our knowledge of prehistoric life. All dinosaurs lived on land and walked on two or four upright legs held directly beneath their bodies. These amazing reptiles are split into two groups. The saurischians, or reptile-hipped dinosaurs, had the two lower bones of the pelvis (the pubis and the ischium) pointing in opposite directions below the pelvic upper bone, or ilium. The ornithischians, or bird-hipped dinosaurs, had pelvic bones with both the pubis and ischium pointing down and back. Dinosaurs appeared about 230 million years ago, and quickly dominated life on land. Their ability to stand upright and move efficiently helped them become versatile and adaptable, but it did not save them from extinction 65 million years ago.

Bony crest

Cheek pouch

Toothless beak

CORYTHOSAURUS
This ornithischian dinosaur belonged to a group called the hadrosaurs that lived 97–65 million years ago in what is now North America, Asia, and Europe. They were plant-eating and had a toothless beak that was similar to that of a duck. However, they had cheek teeth, sometimes more than 300 in each jaw, which they used for grinding tough vegetation. Hadrosaurs probably lived in herds, and their bony crest may have been used as a display for attracting a mate.

Bony frill

Long brow horn

Model of *Triceratops*

Short nose horn

NESTING SITES
The most exciting discoveries of nesting sites have been those in Montana in the United States. The hadrosaur *Maiasaura* ("good mother lizard") laid its eggs in a raised and scooped-out hollow in sand, covering them in vegetation to keep them warm. The 35.5-cm (14-in) long young would have stayed in the nest for a while after hatching and been fed by their parents. *Maiasaura* returned to their nesting colonies from season to season.

TRICERATOPS
This ornithischian dinosaur lived 100 million years ago. It was 1.8–9.1 m (6–30 ft) long and weighed up to 5.4 tonnes. All ornithischian dinosaurs were herbivores, feeding on leaves, fruits, seeds, and even conifer needles. *Triceratops* had a large hooked beak which it used for snipping and tearing at plants, while the teeth of the powerful jaws sheared them. *Triceratops* lived in herds, and used their large defensive horns to see off threats as fierce as *Tyrannosaurus rex*. The bony frill round *Triceratops'* head may have been used to scare predators, attract mates, or simply to protect the neck from attack.

Parrot-like beak

Model of
Baryonyx

Larger brain,
relative to size,
than other dinosaurs

Large, forward-
facing eye

Long, narrow
head

Model of
Troodon

Curved,
pointed tooth

BARYONYX
This unusual carnosaur, or meat-eater, has a long neck,
crocodile-like jaws, and long forelimbs with massive
hooked claws which were probably used for hunting
fish. It was 10 m (33 ft) long and had a rosette of very
large teeth at the tip of its long snout. The rosette
resembles that of today's large
crocodiles. The large
number of smaller,
thin teeth behind the
rosette are more like
those of fish-eating
creatures. The
curved claw could
have been used
for spearing fish.

Sickle-shaped
claw

TROODON
A ferocious, predatory
dinosaur, *Troodon* had a
large, sickle-shaped claw on
its second toe which it used
to slash prey in an attack.
This agile and fleet-footed
saurischian ranged in length
from 1.8–4 m (6–13 ft). It fed on
the vulnerable young or sick from
nesting sites of other dinosaurs, and may even
have laid its own eggs in the same nesting areas.

Reconstruction
of recently dead
Baryonyx based on
fossil find

Model of
Maiasaura
eggs and
hatchlings

Emerging hatchling

Plant material to
protect and keep
eggs warm

Raised nest
of sand

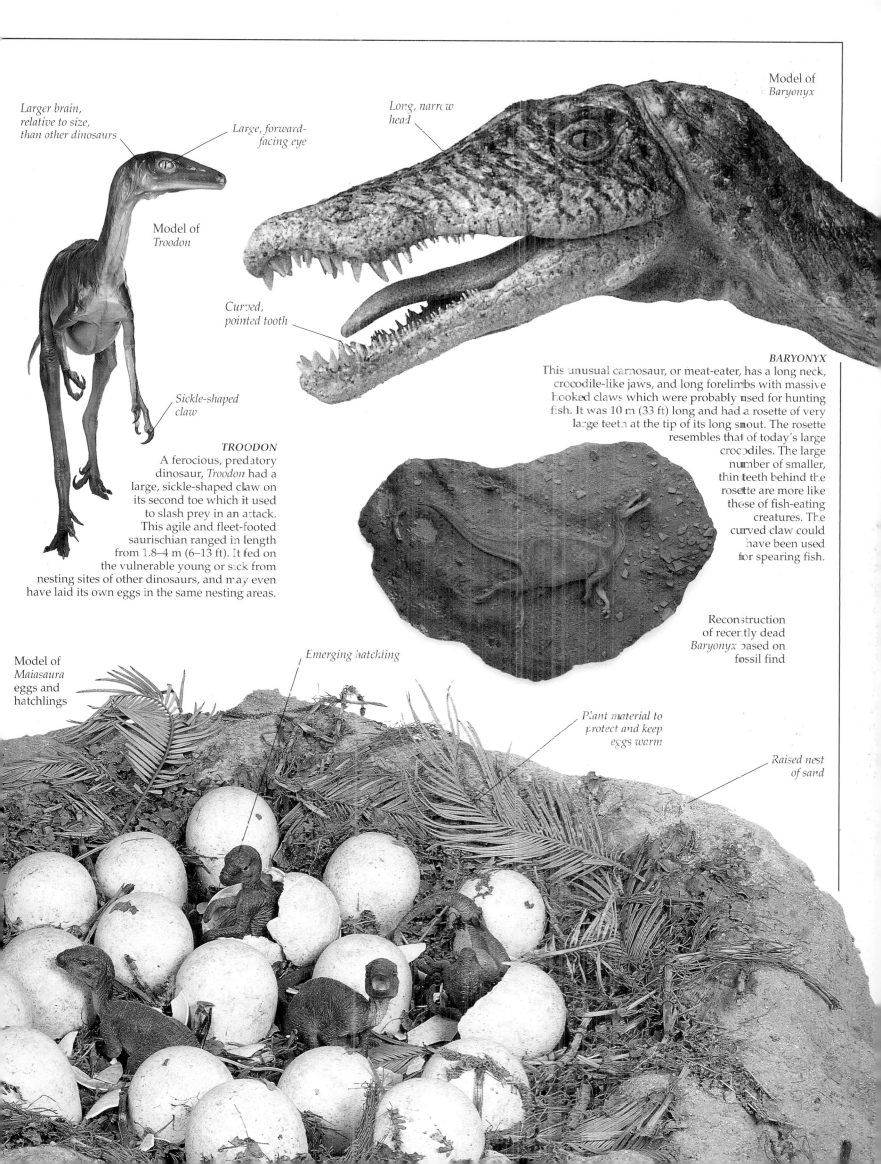

Winged wonders

THE FIRST ANIMALS TO FLY were insects – fossil dragonflies more than 300 million years old have been found in rocks. Flying vertebrates appeared almost 100 million years later, and true flapping flight has evolved in three groups of vertebrates (animals with backbones): the now extinct pterosaurs, living bats, and birds. These creatures are not closely related, and their ability to fly evolved independently. Pterosaurs (the name means "flying lizards") were reptiles, related to dinosaurs, and had a greatly lengthened fourth finger. This supported the fleshy membrane, a thin sheet of muscle and elastic fibres covered by skin, which was the wing. In birds, the feathered wing is supported by several fingers and the lower part of the forearm. Bats are flying mammals and have wings made of a fleshy membrane similar to that of pterosaurs, but supported by four fingers.

WING SUPPORT
This is one of the extended fingerbones which supported the wing of a *Pteranodon*, one of the largest-ever flying animals. The wingspan of this giant pterosaur was an incredible 7 m (23 ft).

WELL-BALANCED
Pteranodon was a pterosaur with a bony crest on its head which counterbalanced its long toothless beak. It appears to have been a fish-eater which soared over the oceans like the albatrosses of today.

BIRDS OF FICTION
The finding of pterosaur remains fuelled the imagination of many authors of science fiction stories.

FURRY REPTILE
The sparrow-sized Jurassic pterosaur *Pterodactylus* had membranous wings, claws, a toothed beak, and a body covered by fine fur. Evidence for fur comes from some pterosaurs which were discovered in Kazakhstan, with hair-like impressions around the body. This may indicate that the pterosaurs were warm-blooded and used their fur as an insulation. The tail of *Pterodactylus* was short, and it had a wingspan of only about 50 cm (20 in), but some pterosaurs had long tails, including *Rhamphorhynchus* with its wingspan of 1.5 m (5 ft).

Toothed beak

Greatly lengthened fourth finger

Membranous wing

Body covered by fine fur

Very short tail

MISTAKEN IDENTITY
This small dinosaur belongs to a group which many scientists believe were ancestors of birds. In 1973, some museum palaeontologists in Germany realized that one of their specimens, identified as *Compsognathus*, was in actual fact an *Archaeopteryx*!

Pterodactylus *had sharp claws for catching and tearing apart prey*

FLYING MAMMAL
It is easy to see the similarity between this bat and the pterosaurs. Because bats often roost in caves, their fossil bones can be found in large numbers in cave deposits.

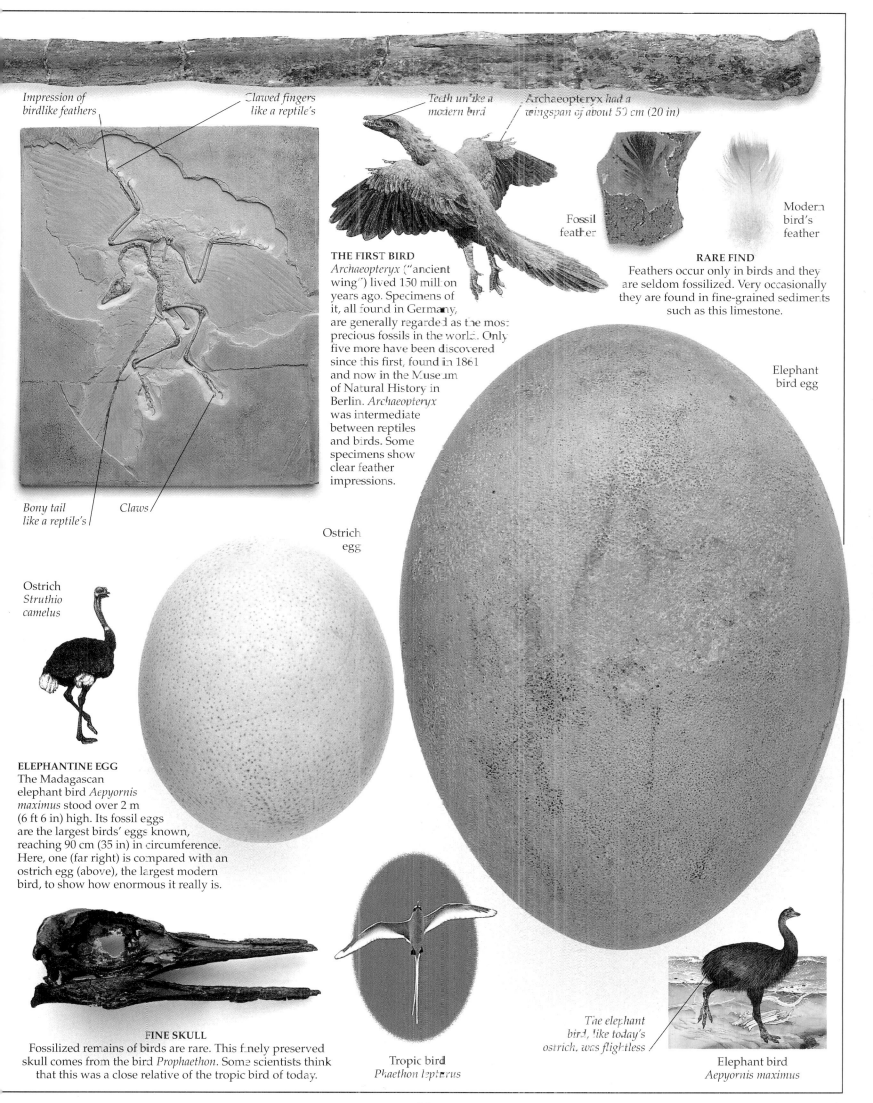

Impression of
birdlike feathers

Clawed fingers
like a reptile's

Teeth unlike a
modern bird

Archaeopteryx had a
wingspan of about 50 cm (20 in)

Fossil
feather

Modern
bird's
feather

THE FIRST BIRD
Archaeopteryx ("ancient
wing") lived 150 million
years ago. Specimens of
it, all found in Germany,
are generally regarded as the most
precious fossils in the world. Only
five more have been discovered
since this first, found in 1861
and now in the Museum
of Natural History in
Berlin. *Archaeopteryx*
was intermediate
between reptiles
and birds. Some
specimens show
clear feather
impressions.

RARE FIND
Feathers occur only in birds and they
are seldom fossilized. Very occasionally
they are found in fine-grained sediments
such as this limestone.

Elephant
bird egg

Bony tail
like a reptile's

Claws

Ostrich
egg

Ostrich
*Struthio
camelus*

ELEPHANTINE EGG
The Madagascan
elephant bird *Aepyornis
maximus* stood over 2 m
(6 ft 6 in) high. Its fossil eggs
are the largest birds' eggs known,
reaching 90 cm (35 in) in circumference.
Here, one (far right) is compared with an
ostrich egg (above), the largest modern
bird, to show how enormous it really is.

FINE SKULL
Fossilized remains of birds are rare. This finely preserved
skull comes from the bird *Prophaethon*. Some scientists think
that this was a close relative of the tropic bird of today.

Tropic bird
Phaethon lepturus

The elephant
bird, like today's
ostrich, was flightless

Elephant bird
Aepyornis maximus

33

The first mammals

WARM-BLOODED MAMMALS have existed for many millions of years. Dwarfed by dinosaurs, the first mammals may have evaded predators because they were very small (rarely larger than rats) and largely nocturnal. Mammals survived the mass extinctions 65 million years ago, and two major groups of mammals are alive today: marsupials and placentals. A third group, the egg-laying, toothless monotremes, has just three species in it, the platypus and two kinds of echidnas. Both marsupials and placentals give birth to live young: marsupial young are immature at birth and develop further in the adult's pouch (pp. 124–125), while placental young are more advanced, having been fed through the placenta inside the mother's womb. Few complete fossilized mammals (pp. 22–23) have survived from prehistoric times, because most mammals died on land, and their remains were scavenged or rotted away. However, if the fresh remains are carried by water into a lake or lagoon and buried in sediment, they did survive. Some mammals have been preserved in tar pits and volcanic ash, and in Siberia and Alaska, well-preserved mammoths have been found frozen in the permafrost.

Bristly fur coat similar to modern hedgehog

Fossils often black in colour because calcium in bones is impregnated with minerals

Scaly plates on tail

Right hind foot

A palaeomastodont, Phiomia, was a predecessor of the elephant

Model of a *Phiomia* based on remains found in Egypt

THE FIRST ELEPHANT
The short-trunked *Phiomia* lived in North Africa about 35 million years ago. It was only 2 m (6 ft 7 in) tall, but it was clearly elephant-like. It had cusped teeth to grind through large volumes of plant food, and the teeth wore down to a flat grinding surface as *Phiomia* became older. In the course of evolution, the second incisor teeth of early elephants grew to become tusks, and as the animals increased in size, the trunk lengthened so it was easier for the animal to eat and drink.

Short tusk for rooting up plants

SUCCESSFUL SURVIVOR

Megazostrodon from South Africa, looked like
a shrew and belonged to a group of tiny
mammals, the morganucodontids, that
lived at the same time as the dinosaurs.
It developed from mammal-like reptiles
more than 200 million years ago. Because it was
covered with hair and could process food rapidly
for energy, *Megazostrodon* could maintain an efficient
body temperature, unlike the sun-bathing reptiles.
However, its body temperature was probably about
25–30°C (75–80°F) – lower than today's mammals.

Model of *Megazostrodon*
found in southern
Africa

*Hind foot was
capable of grasping*

FOSSIL PRESERVATION

This fossil skeleton is of *Pholidocercus*, a primitive
relative of the hedgehog that lived over 49 million
years ago. The skeleton was found in oil shales
in the Messel quarry in Germany, where a
freshwater lake had filled with plant debris,
clay, and dead animals. Horses, anteaters,
primates, and other mammals were
also found in the ancient rocks.
Because there was hardly any
oxygen at the bottom of the
lake, the animals did not
decay completely in the
layers of sediment, so
body outlines, stomach
contents, and even hair
have been fossilized.

Fossil skeleton
of *Pholidocercus*,
found in Germany

Lower jaw

Insect-biting teeth

Neck vertebra

*Front foot with
claws similar
to rat or shrew*

*Pair of large horns
at back of skull*

*Pair of horns
on forehead*

Cast of horned skull
of *Uintatherium*

*Pair of
nasal horns*

Molar tooth

Adult
Uintatherium
with youngster

HERBIVOROUS HORN-HEAD

One of the first large mammals, *Uintatherium*, was the size of an
African rhinoceros, and lived 50 million years ago in North America.
Uintatherium was a hoofed mammal and a herbivore, using its broad,
crested back teeth to slice up stems and leaves, and bark from trees.
Three pairs of horns adorned its skull, the largest pair at the rear and
the smallest on top of the nose. The males also had a pair of large
sabre-like canine teeth. Their elaborate skull ornaments may have
helped to attract mates, or been used for defence and territorial fights.

SUCCULENTS

No plant can survive entirely without water. Plants with fleshy leaves or stems for storing water are known as succulents and include the group of plants called cacti. There are three main kinds of succulent. Stem succulents store water in their stems, and are usually found in the driest climates. Leaf succulents store water in their leaves and grow in damper conditions. Root succulents have thickened roots which serve as water reservoirs.

CHAPTER 2
PLANT LIFE

Many living organisms depend on plants, either
directly or indirectly, to survive. Plants grow in
virtually every habitat on earth, producing oxygen as
a by-product and sustaining all animal life. They are a
source of food and an essential part of all food chains.
After plants have fed, grown, and – many of them –
burst into flower, they then spread their seeds in an
extraordinary and successful variety of ways.

GOLD DUST
The relationship between a plant and
its pollinator (pp. 46–47) is often to
their mutual benefit. A bumblebee
helps carry the gold dust called
pollen from one flower to another,
while it is feeding on the pollen
and sugary nectar which the
flowers produce. The bee
combs the pollen from the
hairs on its body and packs
it into the pollen sacks on
its back legs. It then carries
the pollen back to the nest
where the young bees
feed on the rich protein.

Parts of a plant

THE PART OF A FLOWERING PLANT that grows above the ground is the shoot, which stretches up towards the light. The plant produces flowers that bring about pollination (pp. 46–47) so that seeds can be formed. A flowering plant is supported beneath the soil by a complicated network of roots. The roots anchor the plant and absorb water and minerals from the soil. They are a vital part of a plant's supply system. The leaves of a plant are the main sites for photosynthesis (pp. 40–41) and, via the plant stems, complete the supply system. Some plants also produce rhimzomes, bulbs, corms, tubers, or other reproductive structures. Non-flowering plants, such as ferns and mosses, produce spores.

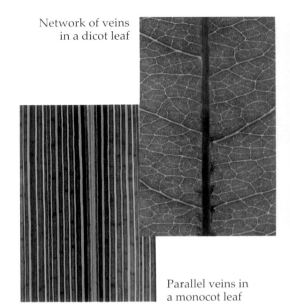

Network of veins in a dicot leaf

Parallel veins in a monocot leaf

LEAF VEINS
Flowering plants are either monocotyledons or dicotyledons. "Monocots" usually have parallel veins in their adult leaves. The adult leaves of "dicots" usually have a network of veins.

FUNGI
Fungi seem to grow like plants, but have no roots or leaves, and produce no seeds. Today, they are classified separately by scientists, but are often described as plants. There are about 100,000 species of fungi in the world.

Lateral root

Midrib

Vein

Root growth happens at tip of each root

Hibiscus
Hibiscus rosa-sinensis

Leaves develop above ground from underground rhizome

UNDERGROUND ROOTS
Rhizomes, tubers, corms, and bulbs are underground storage systems that some plants use to reproduce and survive. Rhizomes are horizontal underground stems that branch out to produce new plants; bulbs are joined swollen leaf bases; corms are swollen stems; and tubers are swollen underground stems.

Brightly coloured tepal attracts insect pollinator

THE SUPPLY SYSTEM
Water, minerals, and sugars are carried up and down a plant in bundles of tube-like cells. One system, called the xylem, carries water and minerals upwards. Another, called the phloem, can carry sugars either upwards or downwards to the parts of the plant that need them.

Large, colourful petals

Stigma

Anther

Filament

FLOWERS
Insects are drawn to a flower by the brightly coloured petals. Once the flower has been pollinated, the petals fall off. The female part of the flower then grows longer to form a capsule which contains the seeds. The seeds are shed when the fully grown capsule opens.

Sepals are small and green

Branch

Stem

Node

Lateral bud

Pedicel (flower stalk)

Flower bud

Petiole (leaf stalk)

Bract (leaf-like structure)

Blade of leaf

A FLOWERING PLANT
The flowering plant hibiscus is a dicotyledon. It has seeds with two seed leaves, or cotyledons, and its leaves are broad with a central midrib and branched veins. Most species of hibiscus in the wild are pollinated by hummingbirds. A hummingbird hovers in front of the flower and inserts its long beak deep inside to reach the nectar. As it feeds, the anthers brush pollen on to its head, while the stigma, also brushing its head, collects pollen from another flower.

39

A light diet

UNLIKE ANIMALS, plants do not need to find food, because they can make it for themselves. The key to the way they do this lies in a green pigment called chlorophyll, which gives all plants their characteristic green colour. By means of chlorophyll, plants can convert energy from sunlight into chemical energy which can be stored, usually in the form of starch. The stored energy is used to fuel the growth and development of the plant. It converts carbon dioxide and water into an energy-rich food compound called glucose, which is then transported through a network of veins to the rest of the plant. This process is known as photosynthesis and it takes place in the leaves of a plant. Many leaves have special adaptations, such as large, flat surfaces, to absorb more sunlight.

Waste product oxygen leaves leaf through stomata

Sunlight is absorbed by chloroplasts in the leaf

Broad, thin blade of leaf suitable for easy absorption of sunlight

Glucose carried to all parts of the plant

Carbon dioxide enters leaf through stomata on lower surface

Water travels to leaf from the roots of the plant

THE PROCESS OF PHOTOSYNTHESIS
Photosynthesis takes place inside special structures called chloroplasts which are found in the leaf cells. The chloroplasts contain the chlorophyll that traps the energy from sunlight. Stomata (pores) in the lower surface of the leaves allow carbon dioxide and oxygen to pass into and out of the plant, while veins carry water into the leaves as well as transporting vital glucose to the rest of the plant.

Leaves produced in the dark have little chlorophyll, and so are pale in colour

Potato tuber kept in dark for six months

Stems grow upwards in search of light and against gravity

A PLANT WITHOUT LIGHT
This potato has spent six months with very little light – a condition that would kill many plants. Because the potato has been in almost complete darkness, it has not been able to produce any food by photosynthesis. However, it has survived and has even produced some roots and shoots. To do this, the young potato shoots have drawn on the food reserves stored by the parent plant during the previous year's growth. The parent plant used the sun's energy to make food, which is stored in the potato tubers mostly in the form of grains of starch. The young potato plants have released energy from the starch and used it for growth.

Each stem is produced by a small bud, or "eye"

Tuber shrinks as food store used up

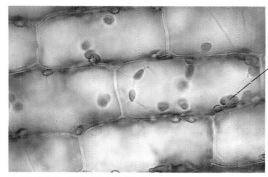

A PLANT'S SOLAR PANELS

Inside the cells that make up a plant's leaves are the tiny structures called chloroplasts. In a single cell, there may be 100 of them. It is inside the chloroplasts that the green, light-trapping pigment chlorophyll is found. The chloroplasts work like minute solar panels, collecting light energy and using it to make food for the plant.

Chloroplast that collects sunlight

Green leaves rich in chlorophyll

New healthier shoots

Potato tuber after three weeks in the light

New shoots

STORING FOOD

Plants store food in various ways – as starches, sugar glucose, or oils. In its first year, an onion plant stores sugars in the onion bulb, which is made up of swollen leaf bases around a shortened stem. In the second year, the sugars in the onion bulb are used up as the plant grows and flowers. The sugars "caramelize", or turn brown, when they are heated strongly, which is why onions darken when fried.

RAPID RECOVERY

Three weeks after emerging from the dark, the potato plant is now growing rapidly, and its leaves have turned green. This has happened because more chlorophyll has been made in the leaves to harness the energy of the sunlight falling on them. The growing potato plant is now able to collect enough light to build up its own reserves and it no longer needs the energy stored in the old tuber. If the potato were now planted, the energy gathered by its leaves would be stored in new potato tubers, and the old tuber would shrivel and die.

Stems now growing rapidly upwards and turning towards the light

Thickening root system with root hairs

A variety of leaves

L EAVES ARE SO VARIED that botanists have invented a whole new language to describe their shapes and the way they grow on plants. One reason for all this variety is that each species of plant needs to adapt to the conditions of its surroundings. A plant living on the gloomy floor of a rainforest may need large leaves to catch enough sunlight. However, a plant growing on a cliff-top has no shortage of light, but is lashed by strong winds, and needs small, strong leaves to survive. Some plants have more than one type of leaf. The leaves of the water crowfoot that are submerged are fine and feathery, so that water can flow past without tearing them. The upper leaves are broad and flat to enable them to float on the surface.

The fine and feathery leaves of water plants prevent them from being damaged by currents in the water

Long, strap-like leaves

CHANGING COLOUR
The leaves of the plant herb Robert gradually change from green to crimson either as the autumn approaches, or in very dry weather.

PARALLEL VEINS
These leaves of a member of the lily family have parallel veins, and they are known as monocot leaves. A network of branch-like veins are found in dicot leaves.

FURRY LEAVES
The leaves of some plants are covered in "fur" which helps to reduce water loss. These leaves are from a pyrethrum which is grown in gardens.

Older leaves

Young leaves

CHANGING SHAPES
The tree of the eucalyptus has two very different shaped leaves. The young stems have round leaves, like coins, and each one completely encircles the thin branch. The leaves on the older parts of the stems have stalks and are shaped like short straps.

FACING THE WIND
Wild asparagus is found on windy coasts. It has flattened branches called cladodes that resemble and function as leaves. The branches are able to withstand the severe gales which would tear fleshy leaves to pieces.

Asparagus
Asparagus officinalis

WATERSIDE GIANTS
Gunneras have enormous leaves – some as big as 2 m (6 ft) in diameter. They grow on riverbanks in tropical forests, but are also found beside water, in warmer parts of temperate countries.

Leaf supported by strong ribs

Underside of a leaf of the herb *Gunnera*

Slashes appear as leaf grows older

Leaflet

Compound leaves are made up of a number of individual leaflets

SLASHED LEAVES
The Swiss cheese plant grows in tropical forests, clinging to trees for support. It probably gets its name from its unusual leaves. With all their slashes and perforations they resemble some types of very holey Swiss cheese.

Simple leaves do not have leaflets

Waxy upper surface

Peltate leaves are shield-shaped, with the stalk coming from the middle

EVERGREEN LEAVES
Evergreen plants do not lose their leaves all at the same time, so they appear green all year round. They need to be tough to survive in the wind, sun, and rain. The leaves of the rhododendron have a thick, waxy surface to prevent them from drying out. They may also have down on their undersides to retain moisture and ward off insects.

Lungwort
Pulmonaria officinalis

Joseph's coat
Amaranthus tricolor

LEAVES OF MANY COLOURS
Variegated, or many-coloured leaves are often found. Lungwort is named after its spotty leaves, which resemble a human lung. The leaves of Joseph's coat are brightly coloured, so the plant is named after the biblical Joseph who wore a multi-coloured coat.

Red underside

Felt-like downy underside

Rhododendron
Rhododendron ponticum

Flowers

THERE IS A PROFUSION of different shapes and colours of flowers that have been produced in the course of evolution. To add to this, people have bred flowers that are even more brilliant or bizarre than those found in the wild. Behind this baffling array of shapes and colours, however, there is a common pattern. For seed production, flowers use the same underlying structure. The male parts, the stamens, produce the pollen. The female parts, the carpels, produce the ovules, which will eventually become the seeds. Around both the male and the female parts are sepals and petals which attract insects, birds, or bats, which will pollinate the flower (pp. 46–47). When, as in the flowers of the lily or clematis, the sepals and petals look the same, they are known as perianth segments, or tepals.

ROUND AND ROUND
The parts of manyflowers are arranged in a circle or whorl. The florets (small flowers) of this sunflower are grouped together to resemble a single, large flower. The outer, yellow ring is made up of ray florets, and surrounds the inner ring of disc florets. Towards the centre of the whorl are the inner, immature disc florets, which appear darker in colour.

Honeysuckle
Lonicera

SCENTED TUBES
Honeysuckle is a shrub with arching branches that use trees and other surfaces to clamber up towards the light. The flower head of this highly scented plant has petals that are fused to form long tubes, a further extension of the plant and one that is very visible and attractive to pollinators.

Sunflower
Helianthus annuus

Nectar produced inside florets

Anther

Disc floret

Ray floret to attract pollinating insects

Stigma

Style

Ovary

Bract

Flattened top of inflorescent stalk

Epidermis, the stalk's outer layer of cells

COMPOSITE FLOWERS
Some plants, such as the tulip, have a single flower. Others, like the dog rose, have lots of flowers, but each one develops and blooms separately. Many other plants produce flowers grouped together in clusters known as flower heads. The flower heads of plants such as sunflowers and daisies are known as composite flowers. This is because they are composed of many tiny flowers clustered together. Sunflower heads have many hundreds of florets – disc florets in the centre of the flower head, and ray florets which each have a single petal-like "ray" around the outer edge.

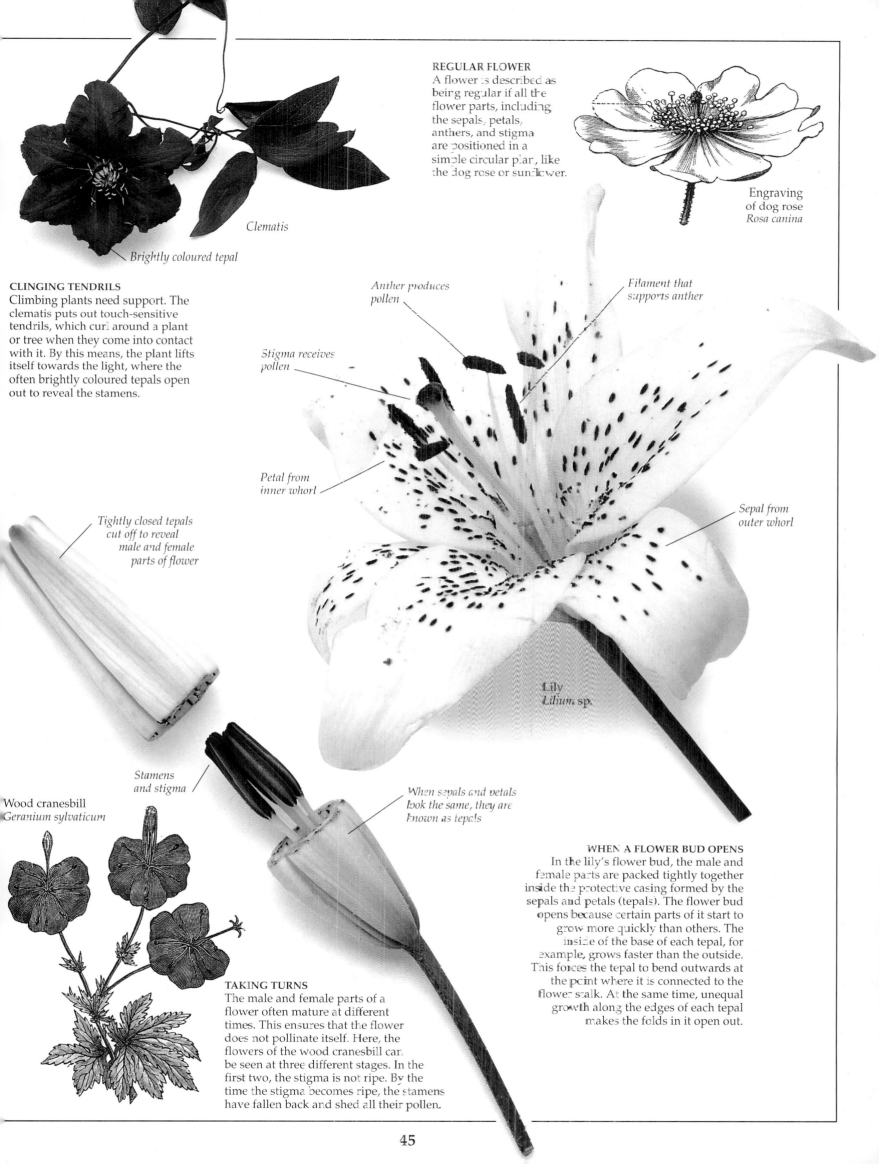

REGULAR FLOWER
A flower is described as being regular if all the flower parts, including the sepals, petals, anthers, and stigma are positioned in a simple circular plan, like the dog rose or sunflower.

Engraving of dog rose
Rosa canina

Clematis

Brightly coloured tepal

CLINGING TENDRILS
Climbing plants need support. The clematis puts out touch-sensitive tendrils, which curl around a plant or tree when they come into contact with it. By this means, the plant lifts itself towards the light, where the often brightly coloured tepals open out to reveal the stamens.

Anther produces pollen

Filament that supports anther

Stigma receives pollen

Petal from inner whorl

Sepal from outer whorl

Tightly closed tepals cut off to reveal male and female parts of flower

Lily
Lilium sp.

Stamens and stigma

When sepals and petals look the same, they are known as tepals

Wood cranesbill
Geranium sylvaticum

WHEN A FLOWER BUD OPENS
In the lily's flower bud, the male and female parts are packed tightly together inside the protective casing formed by the sepals and petals (tepals). The flower bud opens because certain parts of it start to grow more quickly than others. The inside of the base of each tepal, for example, grows faster than the outside. This forces the tepal to bend outwards at the point where it is connected to the flower stalk. At the same time, unequal growth along the edges of each tepal makes the folds in it open out.

TAKING TURNS
The male and female parts of a flower often mature at different times. This ensures that the flower does not pollinate itself. Here, the flowers of the wood cranesbill can be seen at three different stages. In the first two, the stigma is not ripe. By the time the stigma becomes ripe, the stamens have fallen back and shed all their pollen.

45

Pollination

THE EXTRAORDINARY SHAPES and brilliant colours of many flowers have evolved over millions of years to ensure that tiny grains of pollen are carried from one plant to another. Pollen grains have to travel from the male stamens to the female carpels (pp. 44–45) for fertilization to occur. Some plants are able to pollinate themselves (self-pollination), but most rely on receiving pollen from another plant of the same species (cross-pollination). Pollen may be dispersed by wind or by water, but the most important pollinators are insects. Plants entice insects to their flowers with bright colours, and by food in the form of nectar. While the visiting insect feeds, pollen from the anthers at the tops of the stamens is pressed on to the insect's body, often on the back or the head. The stigma of the flower that receives the pollen is in just the right place to collect it as the insect arrives. Some flowers are pollinated by a wide range of insects such as honey-bees, bumblebees, hoverflies, and butterflies. Others rely on a particular pollinator.

Pollen grains magnified many times to show variety of shape

Fine tube to reach ovules, which then develop into seeds

POLLEN GRAINS
Although the largest pollen grains measure only about 0.2 mm across, they have extraordinarily intricate and varied shapes.

Bluebell
Hyacinthoides non-scriptus

Six petals curl back at tip, so pollen sacs are visible

Common toadflax
Linaria vulgaris

Single flower stalks have up to 20 flowers growing on one side of stalk

Bumblebee has long tongue to reach nectar in base of flower

Closed young buds

OPENING UP
The flower of the common toadflax is pollinated by bumblebees. When a visiting bee arrives, the throat of the flower is tightly closed. To reach the nectar at the back of the flower, the bee must open up the flower by pushing forward. The lower petal acts as a landing platform.

FEEDING TIME
As the bumblebee crawls inside in search of the nectar, it brushes against the anthers inside the top of the flower. These dust its back with pollen. The bee feeds on the flower's nectar and any pollen it is already carrying is transferred from its back to the stigma, and the flower is pollinated.

Bright yellow guide marks show bees where to land

Bluebells are usually violet-blue, but can be white or pink

Pollen sacs on stamen

ATTRACTING INSECTS

Insect-pollinated flowers are brightly coloured, scented, and produce nectar, on which the insects feed. These flowers usually have patterns on them which are not visible to the human eye. The patterns can be seen in ultraviolet light (below) and guide a particular insect pollinator, since insects can see ultraviolet.

St John's wort *Hypericum*, under normal light

Dark, central area with nectaries, anthers, and stigmas

Honeyguide

St John's wort under ultraviolet light

INVISIBLE MESSAGES

Insects are attracted to the darkest, central part of the flower, visible in such dark colours here only because it is lit by ultraviolet light. The lines on the petals, the honeyguides, guide the insect to the central part of the flower where it will find pollen and nectar.

Green-veined white butterfly *Pieris napi*

Green colour around veins gives this butterfly its name

BUTTERFLY POLLINATION

Butterflies and moths are also important pollinators but, unlike bees, they do not feed on the pollen and so do not actively collect it. Instead, when they land on a flower to feed on the nectar, pollen from the stamens sticks to their bodies, ready to be carried to the next flower. Because butterflies and moths have a highly developed sense of smell, flowers pollinated by these insects are often scented. Many flower in the late summer when butterflies and moths are most abundant. Butterflies and moths suck up nectar through the proboscis, which is hollow like a drinking straw. The proboscis may vary in length from a fraction of a millimetre to 30 cm (1 ft) long. When not being used, it is coiled up under the butterfly's head.

Also known as wild hyacinths, bluebells have single, thick, supporting stalks

Borne on the wind

ACCORDING TO TRADITION, if you blow on a dandelion's seed head, the number of puffs needed to blow away all the seeds will tell you the time of day. Whether or not this is true, it is a custom that certainly helps the plant to spread. The seeds of the dandelion are encased in tiny fruits and have their own special feathery parachutes to help them float through the air. The dandelion's flower is a composite flower head – in other words, it is composed of many tiny flowers, or florets, clustered together. The tiny florets each produce a single fruit. Like the dandelion, many other composite plants, such as hawkweeds, ragworts, and thistles, rely on the wind to disperse their seeds. The fruits of some of these have parachutes; others have fine hairs that stick out in all directions to form a feathery ball. Many of these plants are troublesome weeds because they quickly colonize bare soil in gardens and on farmland.

Dandelion's tiny fruits float away on the breeze

1 OPENING TIME
The dandelion's flower opens in the morning and closes in the afternoon or when it rains. The plant's name comes from the French *dent de lion*, meaning "lion's tooth", which describes the jagged edges of the leaves.

Flower closes before seeds form

Bracts protect developing seed head

2 THE SEEDS START TO FORM
After opening and closing for a number of days, during which time it may be pollinated, the flower finally closes, and seed formation begins. Gradually the yellow petals wither away, and the "pappus", which is the name given to the small circle of hairs attached to the top of each fruit, starts to grow longer. This is the beginnings of the parachute.

48

Seed head opens
when parachutes
are formed

Bracts
fold back

3 OPENING OUT
The seed head begins to open
only when the weather is dry. At
first, the parachutes are squashed
together, but as the bracts around
the edge of the seed head fold back,
the parachutes begin to expand.

4 READY TO GO
If the air is still, the
fruits may spend several
days attached to the seed
head. This is a dangerous
time for them, because seed-
eating birds like goldfinches are
likely to peck them off and eat them.

Fully
opened
seed head

Parachutes
attached to
tiny fruits

5 LIFT OFF
A slight breeze is all that is needed
to lift the parachutes into the air. They
may fall close by, but with enough
updraught they can be carried for long
distances – 10 km (over 6 miles) is an
average journey for a dandelion seed.
When a fruit lands, it no longer needs
the parachute that has carried it on its
journey, and this breaks off. Over the
winter months, the seeds inside the fruit
sink into the soil, until the spring when
they begin to germinate (pp. 52–53).

Scattering the seed

A PATCH OF BARE GROUND never stays bare for long. Within days, seedlings start to spring up, and if the conditions are right, they eventually cover the ground. Even if the earth is sterilized by heating, so that all the seeds are killed, more somehow arrive and germinate (pp. 52–53). Plants have evolved very effective ways of spreading their seeds, often relying on wind, animals, and water currents. The fruit wall is part of a plant's dispersal method. In certain plants, exploding seed pods fling the seeds into the air; some fruits are winged or cottony to help the seeds become airborne, while other seeds are air-filled and will float on water. Animals also play their part. Many plants have fruits with hooks that stick to fur, and the seeds of some species develop inside tasty berries which are eaten by animals and birds. The seeds pass through these creatures unharmed and fall to the ground where they germinate.

Seed heads
of lotus
*Nymphaea
nucifera*

Seed held
in cup

Dried lotus
head from above

Seed protected
by fruit wall

SPLITTING OPEN
The hard fruit walls of dry fruits such as honesty split open to release their seeds, which are then dispersed by the wind. The edge of the seed coats are flattened to make the seeds more aerodynamic.

Flat edge
of seed
coat

Dry fruit
wall

Honesty
Lunaria annua

Lotuses growing
in ancient Egypt

Long tail for
climbing

Hands used for
manipulating food

Ring-tailed
lemur
*Lemur
catta*

FRUIT-EATER
This ring-tailed lemur lives in tall trees beside rivers in southern Madagascar. Fruit is the most important part of its diet, although it also eats insects and leaves. The seeds of the fruit are spread when the lemur spits them out, lets them fall, or passes them in droppings deposited some distance away from where it found the fruit.

WASHED AWAY
The lotus is a water plant that produces its seeds in a flattened head. When the seeds are ripe, they fall on to the water's surface and float away, carried by the currents until they come to rest on land. Lotus seeds can be extraordinarily long-lived. Some have been known to germinate more than 200 years after they had been shed.

Flower stalk

Exposed seed

Fruit wall enclosing
single seed

TAKING FLIGHT
The fruit wall of some plants, such as the
sycamore (*Acer pseudoplatanus*), splits as it grows,
becoming extended and flattened to form a wing. This
helps the seeds to travel long distances, carried by the wind. The
seeds are carried on their journey inside the fruit wall near the flower stalk.

Flattened wing aids
seed dispersal

Scots pine
Pinus sylvestris

*Mature cone
dropping its
seeds*

PINE CONES
Conifers take a long
time to produce their
seeds, so during
the months that
the seeds are
developing, they are
protected by a hard cone.
In pine trees, the cone falls off
the tree intact some time after the seeds
have been shed. Pine seeds develop in pairs,
with two seeds attached to each scale in the
cone. Each seed has a delicate wing which
is pressed against the scale for protection.

*Tiny, light seeds fall
near parent plant*

Columbine
*Aquilegia
vulgaris*

*Young,
green cones*

*Heavier
poppy seeds
are sprinkled
on the ground*

Opium
poppy
*Papaver
somniferum*

*Closed seed
pod*

Himalayan balsam
Impatiens glandulifera

*Lightweight
fruits with
parachutes,
easily carried
by the wind*

OFF TO A FLYING START
Some plants disperse their seeds
with natural catapults. These work by
suddenly releasing tension that builds
up as the seed case grows. The seed
case splits open, flinging the seeds in all
directions. These catapults are triggered
in a number of ways. Some, particularly
the pods of pea-family plants such as
vetches, burst open when the sun dries
them. Others, such as the Himalayan
balsam, are triggered by movement,
either by the wind blowing past or by
an animal brushing against the plant.

BLOWING IN THE WIND
Seeds that are dispersed by the wind
must be small and light if they are to be
carried any distance by the breeze. When
the wind shakes the seed heads of plants
such as the opium poppy and columbine, the
seeds are scattered just a short distance from
the parent plant. In contrast, when a thistle
seed head catches the wind, its fruits, which
contain the seeds, can be swept high into the
air, sometimes travelling great distances.

Creeping thistle
Cirsium arvense

Prickly leaves

Seeds of life

A SEED IS A TINY, LIFE-SUPPORT package. Inside it is an embryo, which consists of the basic parts from which the seedling will develop or germinate. The food is needed to keep the embryo alive and fuel the process of germination. It is either packed around the embryo, in an endosperm, or stored in special seed leavesknown as cotyledons. For weeks, months, or even years, the seed may remain inactive. But then, when the conditions are right, it suddenly comes alive and begins to grow. During germination, the seed absorbs water, the cells of the embryo start to divide, and eventually the seed coat, or testa, breaks open.

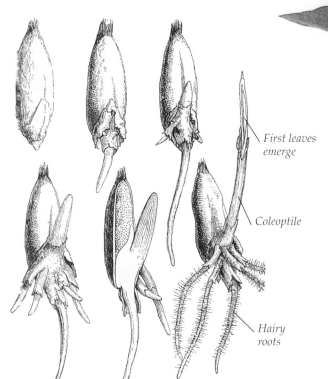

Testa (seed coat)

Cotyledon (seed leaf), where food is stored

Radicle breaking out of testa and growing downwards

First leaves emerge

Coleoptile

Hairy roots

GERMINATING GRAIN
Wheat is a monocot – it has just one seed leaf. The young shoot grows upwards through the soil, protected by a tube called a coleoptile. The growing point of the leaves of the wheat plant is at ground level and can continue to produce new shoots at the base even if the leaves are removed.

First true leaves emerging

Plumule (shoot) straightening towards light

Developing runner bean
Phaseolus coccineus

Root hairs absorb water and salt from soil

FIRST GROWTH
Germination is the growth of seeds into seedlings. It begins when seeds become active below ground, and ends when the first foliage leaves appear above ground. When the seeds have dispersed from the parent plant, they dehydrate and lie dormant, sometimes for many months. Then they begin to germinate into seedlings, provided they have enough water, oxygen, warmth, and, in some cases, light. First, the seed takes in water and the embryo begins to use its food store. The beginnings of the root system, or radicle, sprouts, breaks through the seed coat, or testa, and grows downwards.

Broad bean
Vicia faba
root breaking through seed coat

REACHING THE LIGHT
As the plumule grows longer, it breaks above ground. Once through the soil, it straightens up towards the light, and the first trueleaves appear. In the runner bean (above) and thebroad bean (left), the seed leaves stay buried.This is known as "hypogeal" germination. With the opening of the first true leaves, the seedling starts to produce its own food by photosynthesis (pp. 40–41).

First true leaves
open out

Testa
(seed coat)

Testa
(seed coat)

Plumule
(embryonic
shoot)

Hypocotyl
section of
root growth

Cotyledon
(seed leaf)

Pore for
water
absorption

Lateral
root

REPRODUCTION
Once germination is complete,
the runner bean grows quickly.
Because it is a climbing plant, it
does not need to develop thick
stems. Instead, it uses other
plants for support. Given the
right conditions, the plant will
produce its first flowers in about
six weeks. After pollination
(pp. 46–47) and fertilization, the
flowers will develop into long
pods full of seeds. By the time
the seeds have dried out, the life
cycle of the runner bean has
come full circle.

Fully upright stem

Black bean
Phaseolus sp.
seed at start of
germination

Cross-section
of black bean
showing radicle
that has broken
through testa and
lengthened

Seed case is no
longer needed and
starts to shrivel

PLANT DIVERSITY
Flowering plants are either
monocotyledons, like the
wheat plant, or dicotyledons,
like the runner bean and black
bean. Dicotyledons have seeds
with two cotyledons (above),
their leaves are broad, with a
central midrib and branched
veins, and their flower parts
are usually in multiples of four
or five, whereas monocots
usually have flowers in
multiples of three.

Elongated
primary root

Thick mass of roots
to absorb water
and nutrients

DEVELOPING ABOVE GROUND
The black bean is a plant that has "epigeal"
germination, which means the seed leaves are lifted
above ground. There, they turn green and start to
produce food for the seedling. The seed leaves are
pushed up by growth in the middle section of the
root, the hypocotyl. The radicle still breaks through
the testa as in hypogeal plants (the seed leaves
of which develop below the ground), but the
primary root of an epigeal plant gets very long.

FIERCE FEEDER
In a typical food chain, the lion is the top predator. The adult male may eat 40 kg (90 lb) of meat in a sitting, although he may not feed again for several days. The lionesses in a group of lions, or pride, do most of the hunting, sometimes two or more of them stalking and killing the antelope or zebra that is the main food of the group.

CHAPTER 3

ANIMAL LIFE

THERE IS AN INCREDIBLE VARIETY of animal life in
the world, from brightly-coloured beetles and many-
legged centipedes, to waddling penguins and writhing
snakes, scuttling brown rats and fierce polar bears.
The variety is reflected in their lifestyles, although
they have all developed ingenious ways of protecting
and feeding themselves and their young.

LAYING IN STORES
Female butterflies and moths lay batches
of eggs on the plants that will provide
food for the caterpillars when they hatch
(pp. 60–61). The caterpillar is a voracious
and continuous feeder, eating and
growing larger until it pupates. In the
pupa, or chrysalis (pp. 58–59), the insect
develops further until it eventually
emerges as a fully grown butterfly.

Insect life

INSECTS ARE THE MOST ABUNDANT creatures on earth – over five million species. They first appeared 300 million years ago and were the first animals to fly. All insects have six legs, and their skeleton is on the outside of their body. This outer skeleton, or exoskeleton, forms a soft, protective covering round the vulnerable internal organs. A young insect is called a larva. As each larva feeds and grows, it must shed its hard exoskeleton. When the larva grows too large, the exoskeleton splits, revealing a new skin underneath. Most insects have two pairs of wings, each with a network of veins to give strength to their structure. Insects use antennae, or feelers, to investigate their surroundings. Some insects have very long antennae which they use mainly for touch. Others have antennae that sense airborne chemicals, sometimes in minute quantities. Antennae that do this are often feathery, which gives them a large surface area for collecting scent molecules from the air.

Back legs pulled in to push insect into air

JUMPING INSECTS
Grasshoppers, crickets, and locusts are all powerful jumpers. They bring the long, slender parts of their hind legs close under the body. The large muscles shorten, or contract, and the legs are suddenly straightened, throwing the insect into the air.

DANGER ON EIGHT LEGS
Although many people think they are, spiders are not insects. This red-kneed tarantula, *Brachypelma smithi*, stays in its silk-lined burrow during the day, emerging after dark to hunt for large insects or small invertebrates.

PART OF A LARGE FAMILY
There are about 170,000 known species of moths and butterflies in the world. Together the two groups make up one group known as the Lepidoptera, from the Greek words for "scale" and "wing".

Orange albatross
Appias nero

CONTROL IN THE AIR
Dragonflies are among the most accomplished fliers in the insect world. They can hover, fly fast or slow, change direction rapidly, and even fly backwards. As they manoeuvre, their two pairs of wings beat independently of each other. Dragonflies can often be seen hovering above water, ready to dart away after the insects on which they feed. The young dragonflies, or nymphs, show no sign of wings, but older nymphs develop buds on the thorax, inside which the adult wings develop.

Compound eye

Hindwing

Forewing

Unlike most insects, a dragonfly cannot fold its wings

LIVING FOOD

Many insects practise a form of parasitism that involves laying eggs on or in another insect, which then acts as a living store of food for the insect's grubs to feed on. This striped field digger wasp is paralyzing a fly which it will carry back to its nest for her grubs to eat. Insects that carry out this kind of parasitism, or indirect predation, can be used by humans to keep down the population numbers of pests that attack many economically important crops. It is a natural form of biological control, which is less harmful than the use of poisonous chemicals.

Long antenna helps insect locate prey

Surfaces of thorax pulled closer together

Wing moves up

MOVING UP

When an insect flies, most of the power for flapping the wings is provided by large muscles in the thorax. The vertical muscle contracts, making the wings move up.

Striped field digger wasp
Mellinus arvensis

Thorax

Wing moves down

MOVING DOWN

When the horizontal muscle in the thorax contracts, the upper and lower surfaces of the thorax are driven apart, causing the wings to move down. Other muscles at the base of the wings adjust the angle of each stroke, and thus determine the direction of flight.

Field digger wasp holds prey tightly

Housefly
Musca domestica

Houseflies only have two wings

Feathery antennae can sense air movements

WARMING UP

An insect's flight muscles must be warm before the wings can be moved fast enough for flight. Beetles may open and shut their elytra (wing cases) several times before taking flight. The cockchafer beetle launches itself into the air from the top of a plant and faces into the wind. The hind wings provide propulsion during flight, and the hardened elytra that protect the fragile hind wings assist by providing lift, like the wings of an aeroplane.

Wing joint unfolding ready to take flight

Cockchafer beetle
Melolontha melolontha

Insect transformation

METAMORPHOSIS MEANS "change of body form and appearance". The most advanced insects have a complex life-cycle involving "complete" metamorphosis. The eggs hatch to produce larvae (caterpillars, grubs, or maggots) that are quite unlike adult insects in both form and appearance. The larvae grow and moult several times, finally producing a pupa, or chrysalis. Inside the pupa, the whole body is reorganized, and a winged adult produced. This life-cycle enables the larvae to specialize in feeding, and the adults to specialize in breeding and looking for new sites. Wasps, bees, ants, flies, beetles, butterflies and moths, caddis flies, lacewings, fleas, and scorpion flies all undergo complete metamorphosis. Grasshoppers, cockroaches, termites, mayflies, dragonflies, and many bugs undergo "incomplete" metamorphosis. Like the original primitive insects, they transform gradually through a series of stages, the nymphs becoming more and more like the adults. There is no pupal stage in this process.

MATING
Mexican bean beetles (*Epilachna varivestis*) are a species of plant-feeding ladybird beetle. The adult males and females look very similar and mate frequently.

EGGS
Female Mexican bean beetles glue their eggs in groups of about 50 to the underside of leaves where the eggs will be well protected. Each egg stands on its end and takes about seven days to hatch.

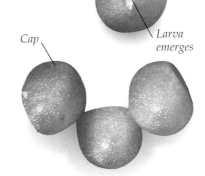

Cap

Larva emerges

1 EGG HATCHES
Even eggs have to breathe. Around the top of each egg is a ring of pores which allow air to reach the developing larva inside. About a week after the egg has been laid, the cap at the top is broken or chewed off, and the larva emerges.

Old larval skin

New pupal skin

4 ABOUT TO CHANGE
When the larva has eaten enough food, it attaches itself to the under-side of a damaged, netted leaf, ready to pupate. The larval skin is shed, and soft new pupal skin forms beneath it. This quickly hardens.

Larva feeding on plant shoot

DIET OF LEAVES
Mexican bean beetles feed on leaves both as larvae and adults. Because they only eat the fleshy parts in between the veins, the leaf becomes netted and lacy.

Old larval skin with long spines

New pupal skin with short spines

Dead, lacy leaves on which larvae have fed

5 RESTING
A pupa is often called a "resting stage". But there is no rest for all the cells in the insect's body. The muscles, nerves, and other structures are dissolved, and new limbs, with new muscles and nerves, are formed. In this picture, the smooth yellow of the adult beetle's wing cases and the first segment of the thorax can be seen through the thin, transparent, spiny skin of the pupa.

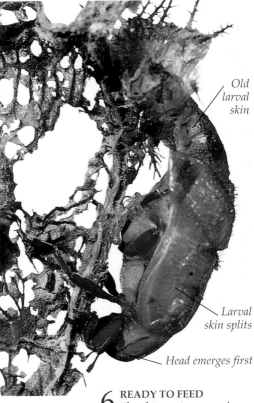

Old larval skin

Larval skin splits

Head emerges first

6 READY TO FEED
The thin, spiny pupal skin splits along the underside, and the smooth young adult slowly draws itself free, headfirst. It takes the young beetle about one hour from the splitting of the pupal skin to free itself fully.

STAG BEETLE DEVELOPMENT
The larvae of stag beetles and other scarab beetles always adopt a C-shaped posture. The male pupa is easy to distinguish from the female pupa by its large jaws.

Eggs

Young larva

Mature larva

Male pupa

Female pupa

Pupa

Larva

SCORPION FLIES
Scorpion flies have a complete metamorphosis. This drawing shows a larva, and a pupa with well-developed wing buds.

A MAN TRANSFORMED
This painting by Barbara Lofthouse depicts a scene from Franz Kafka's story *Metamorphosis*, in which a man changes into an insect.

Red spots are associated with simple eyes

Soft spines harden quickly

Emerging larva

PROTECTION FROM PARASITES
The spines on the surface of the larvae are branched, with hard, pointed tips. Spines like this are found on the larvae of all plant-feeding ladybirds, but not on any of the more common predatory species. The spines make the larvae unpleasant for bird predators and may deter parasites from laying eggs.

2 LARVA EMERGES
As the soft-spined larva crawls out of its egg, three red pigment spots can be seen on either side of the insect's head. Larvae do not have compound eyes, like adults, and these spots are associated with simple eyes.

3 A FIRST MEAL
In many insect species, as soon as a young larva is free from its egg, it eats the shell, which contains valuable nutrients. The soft spines on the surface of the larva's body quickly harden.

Old larval skin remains attached to leaf

7 SPOTLESS
Immediately after it has emerged, the young beetle is yellow and has no spots, although the wing cases quickly harden. Before the beetle can fly away, there is a crucial stage that can last up to two to three hours. The young beetle holds its wing cases up and expands the wings below to allow them to dry.

Young adult

8 ONE MORE PEST
After about 24 hours the adult spots appear on the wing cases, but the copper colour takes about seven to ten days to develop fully. About 100 years ago, this species spread slowly northwards from Mexico on plots of *Phaseolus* beans. Then, in 1918, it was accidentally imported to the eastern United States and spread rapidly towards Canada. Today, it is a serious pest in bean crops in North and Central America, although it still cannot live in central areas because of the harsher winters.

59

An emerging caterpillar

BUTTERFLIES AND MOTHS usually lay large numbers of eggs. The amount laid at one time varies greatly; some females lay over 1,000 eggs, although of those only a few may survive to become adults. Eggs also vary from one species to another in colour and in surface texture, which can be smooth or beautifully sculptured. The two main types are a flattened oval shape, usually with a smooth surface, and a more upright shape, which often has a heavily ribbed surface. In many cases, the female lays the eggs on a leaf or stem, but species that feed on a wide variety of plants often scatter their eggs in flight. Both methods are designed to place the caterpillar as near as possible to the plant on which it feeds. On these two pages, the caterpillar of a South American Owl butterfly, *Caligo idomeneus* hatches from its egg.

THE EGGS IN POSITION
The South American Owl butterfly lays its eggs in groups. The colour of the individual eggs can vary in this species. The eggs turn darker in colour (top right) as the time of hatching approaches.

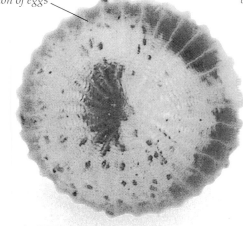

Pattern of ridges can be useful aid to identification of eggs

1 RESTING
The autumn-laid eggs of many temperate butterflies and moths usually go into a resting stage called "diapause". This means that they can survive the winter months. This state is broken by warm or fluctuating temperatures.

Darker colour shows egg will soon be ready to hatch

2 WARMING UP
Diapause is broken when the temperature has risen enough for the caterpillar to stand a chance of survival after the winter months. The egg darkens in colour as the tiny caterpillar gets ready to emerge.

3 CUTTING A CIRCLE
In order to hatch, the caterpillar must bite its way through the shell of the egg. This is not a hard, brittle shell like that of a bird's egg, but it is still a tough task for the tiny caterpillar. Its jaws have to cut a circle big enough for the head to emerge, so it has enormous mouthparts.

Head of caterpillar starting to appear

Opening where caterpillar's jaws have cut through shell

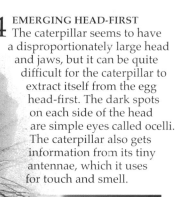

Ocellus

4 EMERGING HEAD-FIRST
The caterpillar seems to have a disproportionately large head and jaws, but it can be quite difficult for the caterpillar to extract itself from the egg head-first. The dark spots on each side of the head are simple eyes called ocelli. The caterpillar also gets information from its tiny antennae, which it uses for touch and smell.

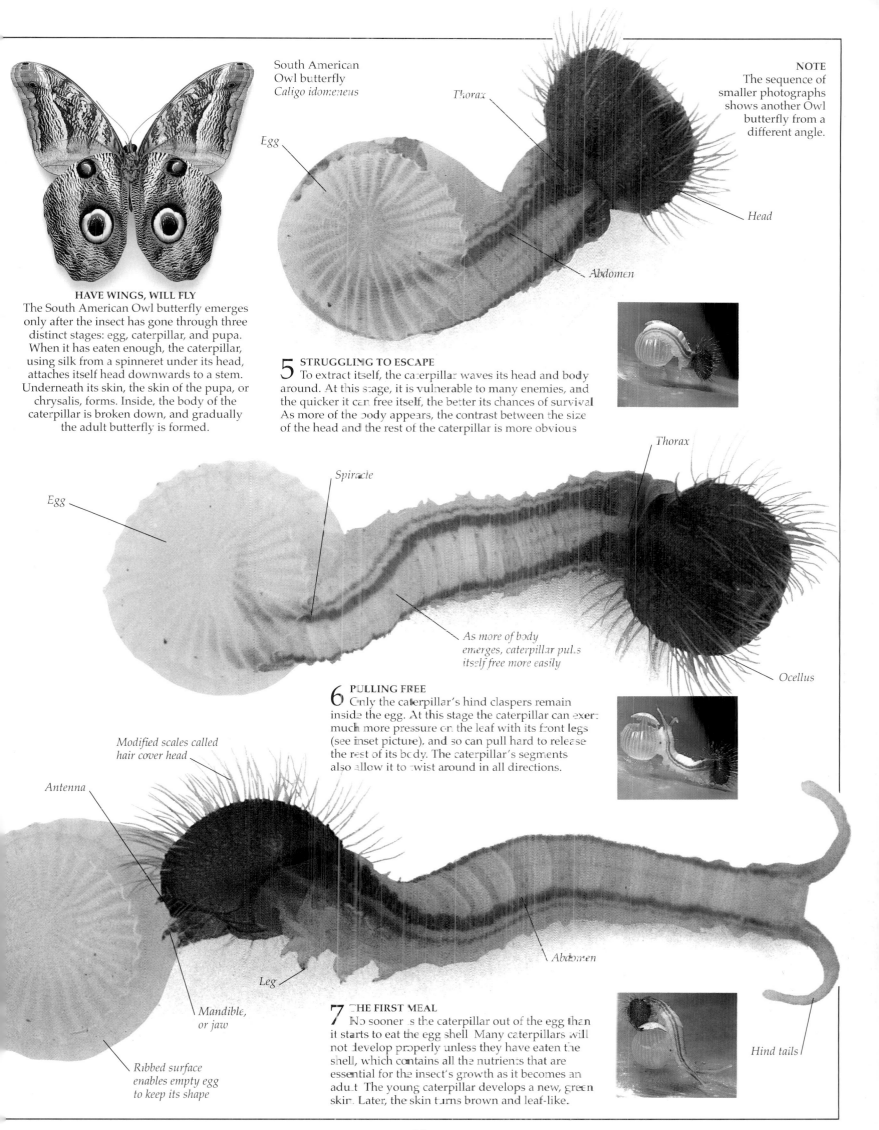

South American
Owl butterfly
Caligo idomeneus

Thorax

Egg

Head

Abdomen

HAVE WINGS, WILL FLY
The South American Owl butterfly emerges
only after the insect has gone through three
distinct stages: egg, caterpillar, and pupa.
When it has eaten enough, the caterpillar,
using silk from a spinneret under its head,
attaches itself head downwards to a stem.
Underneath its skin, the skin of the pupa, or
chrysalis, forms. Inside, the body of the
caterpillar is broken down, and gradually
the adult butterfly is formed.

5 STRUGGLING TO ESCAPE
To extract itself, the caterpillar waves its head and body
around. At this stage, it is vulnerable to many enemies, and
the quicker it can free itself, the better its chances of survival.
As more of the body appears, the contrast between the size
of the head and the rest of the caterpillar is more obvious.

Spiracle

Thorax

Egg

*As more of body
emerges, caterpillar pulls
itself free more easily*

Ocellus

6 PULLING FREE
Only the caterpillar's hind claspers remain
inside the egg. At this stage the caterpillar can exert
much more pressure on the leaf with its front legs
(see inset picture), and so can pull hard to release
the rest of its body. The caterpillar's segments
also allow it to twist around in all directions.

*Modified scales called
hair cover head*

Antenna

Abdomen

7 THE FIRST MEAL
No sooner is the caterpillar out of the egg than
it starts to eat the egg shell. Many caterpillars will
not develop properly unless they have eaten the
shell, which contains all the nutrients that are
essential for the insect's growth as it becomes an
adult. The young caterpillar develops a new, green
skin. Later, the skin turns brown and leaf-like.

Leg

*Mandible,
or jaw*

Hind tails

*Ribbed surface
enables empty egg
to keep its shape*

Anatomy of a butterfly

BUTTERFLIES AND MOTHS are unique among insects in that every part of their body, from their wings to their feet, is covered with thousands of delicate scales. The most noticeable scales are those covering the upper and under surfaces of the wings, as these give the butterfly its colour and pattern. The head has two jointed sensory organs called antennae, used for smelling, and a specialized coiled feeding tube, or proboscis, that uncoils when the insect wishes to feed. The two large compound eyes are made up of a large number of individual lenses, or facets. The facets are sensitive not only to movement, but also to the colour patterns of flowers and other butterflies. Divided into three segments, the thorax is the powerhouse of the body, with connecting muscles for the two pairs of wings and the three pairs of segmented legs. The insect's reproductive organs are in the tip of the abdomen, the rest of which contains most of its digestive system.

A Clouded Yellow, *Colias croceus*, in flight

FEEDING HABITS

All butterflies and most moths have a hollow feeding tube called a proboscis which they use for drawing up energy-rich nectar, water, and other liquids. A few large moths do not feed as adults, but live on food stored up by the larva. There are species of butterflies who enjoy sipping the juice of rotting fruit or the sap oozing from trees; others eat honey dew, or the liquids from dead animal carcasses.

Labial palps for testing suitability of food

Front of butterfly head

Proboscis

Detail of proboscis

Fritillary butterflies, belonging to the Nymphalidae family

Head of a Pearl-bordered Fritillary, *Clossiana euphrosyne*, Europe

Compound eye

Labial palps

Coiled proboscis

THE "TONGUE"
The proboscis of a butterfly is situated underneath the head. The hollow feeding tube acts like a coiled drinking straw.

A DRINK AT THE CLUB
It is quite common, especially in hot climates, to see a group of male butterflies drinking from damp soil – possibly to obtain the minerals. The majority of the butterflies in this "mud puddle" club are Blue triangle butterflies, or Bluebottles, from Malaysia.

Scarce swallowtail, *Iphiclides podalirius*, Europe and Asia

Forewing

Hindwing

Thorax

Abdomen

Antenna

AT REST
This engraving shows a Scarce swallowtail resting in a typical swallowtail position, with its wings folded up above its body

Rows of scales form the patterns and colours

Homerus swallowtail, *Papilio homerus*, Jamaica

A LARGE FAMILY
The Homerus swallowtail, only found in Jamaica and an endangered species because of its popularity with collectors, is one of 500 species belonging to a large family of butterflies, the Papilionidae, that contains some of the most beautiful butterflies in the world. Most of the species are found in the tropics, and are strong fliers. They have large wings and three fully developed pairs of legs. Swallowtails get their name from the tapered shape of their hindwings.

WHICH FAMILY?
The veins in the wings of butterflies and moths help to keep the wing in the correct flight position. The way the veins are arranged also helps identify the family to which a species belongs.

COMING IN TO LAND
With its wings slightly curved, this Peacock butterfly is about to land on a buddleia. Butterflies have enormous control over their flight movements and can make sudden landings with ease.

Spinning silk

Illustrations from *Vermis sericus*, a popular 17th-century book on silkmoths

SILK IS PRODUCED by the caterpillars of most moths, but the finest quality silk is made by species of moths in the families Saturniidae and Bombycidae. In particular, it is made by the caterpillars of the large white moth, *Bombyx mori*, more commonly known as the Chinese silkworm. Today, this silkworm has become so domesticated that it no longer occurs in the wild. According to Chinese legend, silk fibre was first discovered as early as 2700 BC. However, for centuries the methods used to produce silk commercially were kept a well-guarded secret and the export of silkworms or their eggs out of China was a crime punishable by death. Despite this, silkworm eggs, and the seeds of the mulberry trees on which the caterpillars feed, were eventually smuggled out of China, possibly hidden in a walking stick. In Europe, silk had been a highly valued material in the making of luxurious clothing for a long time. Even when the Arabs introduced silkworms into Spain, and silk-weaving centres had been set up in Italy, silk continued to command high prices.

REELING OF THE COCOONS
The production of silk originated in China. This 19th-century engraving shows the thread being transferred on to smaller bobbins as it becomes finer. The bobbins of silk were then dyed before being used to weave rich cloth. Today, silk-making is more mechanized, but the basic process remains the same.

UNWINDING THE THREAD
In 17th-century Europe, the methods used to produce silk changed little. The insects inside the cocoons were killed in boiling water before they could hatch. This prevented them breaking the thread of silk and also dissolved the gum-like substance which held the strands together. The threads from several cocoons were then caught up and twisted together.

Thread was wound on to a reel or frame

3 BUILDING UP THE WALLS
As the caterpillar works backwards and forwards between the leaves, the cocoon is made thicker. A fine thread of silk is forced out through the spinneret.

1 FINDING A SITE

The caterpillar of the silkworm finds a suitable site surrounded by leaves before beginning to spin silk. The silk is produced by glands in the caterpillar's body and comes out through the spinneret under its head.

Silk thread is attached to surrounding leaves

2 THE EARLY STAGES

The caterpillar spins a small web, weaving the silken thread into a loose cocoon. At this point, the network of the cocoon is not very dense, so the caterpillar is still clearly visible to the naked eye.

If a single thread of silk is unravelled, it measures about 805 m (0.5 miles) long

Dense walls of silk

4 INCREASING THE DENSITY

The thickness of the silk layer increases, and the cocoon is now established and strong enough to keep most parasites and predators away from the changing caterpillar.

5 A SAFE HAVEN

Pupae are vulnerable to predators because they cannot move about. The best strategy of survival is for the pupa to adopt the shape and colour of its surroundings until the insect emerges as a moth.

Fully protected caterpillar can now begin to pupate

Moths in flight

THERE ARE AT LEAST 170,000 different species of butterflies and moths, but nine-tenths of these are moths. The German word for moths, *nachtschmetterlinge* ("night-butterflies"), reflects the popular view of their behaviour. While it is true that the majority of moths fly at dusk or during the night, quite a large number fly by day. Although moths such as the silkworm (pp. 64–65) are useful to people, a few species are harmful. These include the moths that destroy crops, fruit, or trees; the clothes moths that damage woollen goods; and moths that spread diseases in cattle by feeding on the moisture around their eyes. The majority of moths are harmless, pollinating flowers and forming a vital part of the complex web of life.

Old engraving showing main parts of a moth; the darker lines represent part of the wing pattern

Darwin's hawkmoth, *Xanthopan morgani*

THE LONGEST TONGUE?
This amazing proboscis belongs to Darwin's hawkmoth, from Madagascar. The celebrated English naturalist, Charles Darwin (1809–82), knew of a Madagascan orchid which had its nectar at the base of a 30-cm (12-in) corolla. As the orchid obviously needed to be pollinated, Darwin thought there must be a moth with a proboscis that measured 30 to 33 cm (12 to 13 in) in length. Years later, the discovery of the hawkmoth proved Darwin's theory correct.

Feeding

Like butterflies, most moths take nectar from flowers. Day-flying moths often hover in front of a flower as they feed. Many large moths do not feed at all as adults. During its short adult life, the Indian moon moth (right and below) lives entirely off food stored in its body during the caterpillar stage.

FINDING NECTAR
The long proboscis of the hawkmoth is used to seek out nectar. During the probing, pollen is picked up and transferred from flower to flower.

Eye

Eye

Labial palp

Proboscis

MOTH HEAD
In a moth's head (right) the brain receives information about its environment from the eyes, antennae, and sense organs called palps.

Characteristic thick body and long forewings of all hawkmoths. This group of moths are all powerful fliers

FACE-TO-FACE WITH A MOTH
An almost head-on view of the Indian moon moth shows its antennae, as well as its front and middle legs. The antennae have minute sense organs that probably detect not only scent but also changes in air pressure.

Female uses its antennae to select correct food plant on which to lay eggs

No proboscis because Indian moon moth does not feed as an adult

Trailing tails helps protect this moth

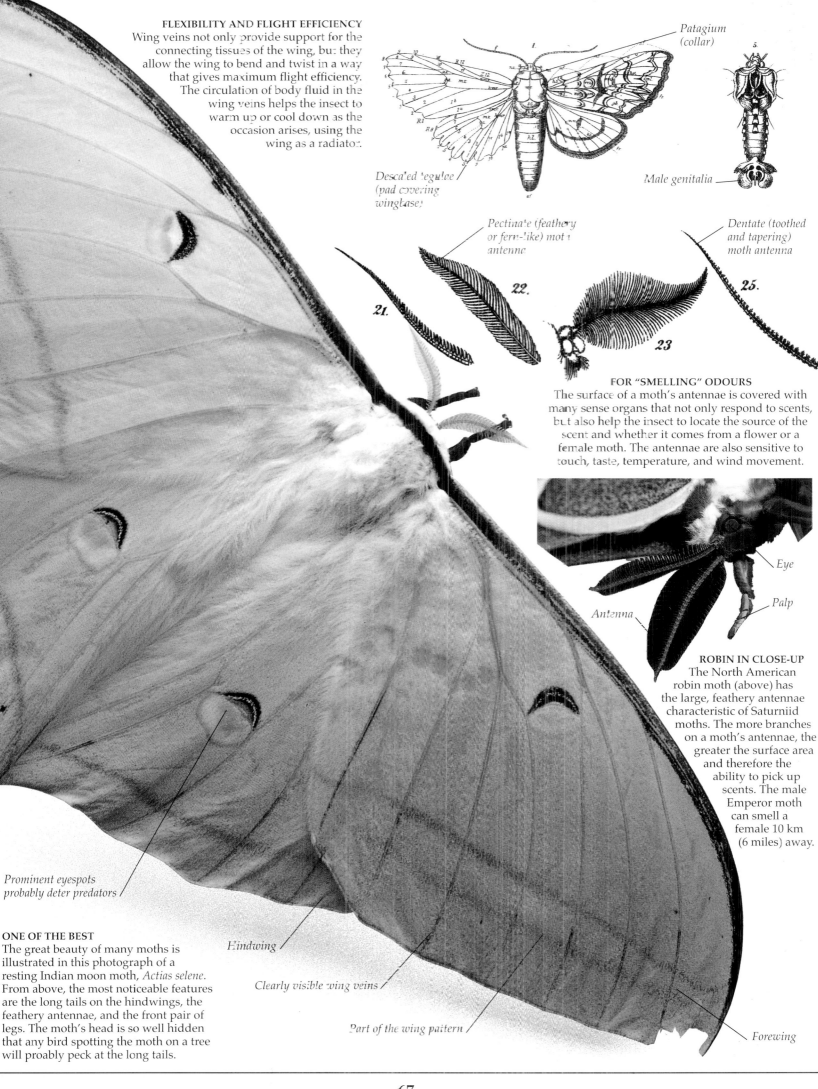

FLEXIBILITY AND FLIGHT EFFICIENCY
Wing veins not only provide support for the connecting tissues of the wing, but they allow the wing to bend and twist in a way that gives maximum flight efficiency. The circulation of body fluid in the wing veins helps the insect to warm up or cool down as the occasion arises, using the wing as a radiator.

Patagium (collar)

Descaled tegulae (pad covering wingbase)

Male genitalia

Pectinate (feathery or fern-like) moth antenna

Dentate (toothed and tapering) moth antenna

21.

22.

23.

25.

FOR "SMELLING" ODOURS
The surface of a moth's antennae is covered with many sense organs that not only respond to scents, but also help the insect to locate the source of the scent and whether it comes from a flower or a female moth. The antennae are also sensitive to touch, taste, temperature, and wind movement.

Eye

Palp

Antenna

ROBIN IN CLOSE-UP
The North American robin moth (above) has the large, feathery antennae characteristic of Saturniid moths. The more branches on a moth's antennae, the greater the surface area and therefore the ability to pick up scents. The male Emperor moth can smell a female 10 km (6 miles) away.

Prominent eyespots probably deter predators

ONE OF THE BEST
The great beauty of many moths is illustrated in this photograph of a resting Indian moon moth, *Actias selene*. From above, the most noticeable features are the long tails on the hindwings, the feathery antennae, and the front pair of legs. The moth's head is so well hidden that any bird spotting the moth on a tree will proably peck at the long tails.

Hindwing

Clearly visible wing veins

Part of the wing pattern

Forewing

Homes with hinges

BIVALVES ARE AMONG the best known of all marine creatures. They are molluscs, but their shells are divided into two parts, or valves, that completely enclose and protect the soft body of the mollusc inside. The valves are connected by a shell-like ridge or teeth that form a hinge, and can be opened and closed by strong muscles and ligaments. Bivalves do not lead very active lives – unable to extend far out of their shells to crawl, many live embedded in sand and mud, or remain hidden in rock crevices, while others attach themselves to a hard surface. They feed by opening their valves and filtering water through their gills to catch tiny creatures in the water around them. Bivalves occur in vast numbers – as many as 8,000 living shells are sometimes found in one square metre of the sea floor.

THE BIRTH OF VENUS
This detail from the famous painting by Botticelli shows the birth of Venus from a scallop shell.

Royal cloak scallop

SCURRYING SCALLOPS
Scallops are very common bivalve molluscs. Some scallops are uniquely able to open and close their valves to swim away rapidly when disturbed.

Pacific thorny oyster

Spiky exterior

Ligament

SPINY SHELL
Spiny, or thorny, oysters are also known as chrysanthemum shells because of their likeness to the spiky-petalled flowers. Although not related to the true oyster, they are similar in that they remain attached to a solid base throughout their lives.

BUTTERFLY WINGS
Shiny, colourful tellin shells are often washed ashore still in pairs resembling butterfly wings.

BEAN CLAMS
Generally tiny and wedge-shaped, these creatures live in large numbers on warm-water beaches. Being so abundant, they are often used as food, especially in soups.

Noble pen
shell

GIANT BATH
The enormous
tridacna shell houses
an animal that can feed
up to 20 people! Common
in the Molucca Islands,
the shell can be used
as a child's bathtub.

THE GIANT PEN SHELL
The pinna, or pen shell,
spends its life in an upright
position with its tapered end
semi-embedded in soft bases,
usually among weeds. The
giant pen shell, which lives in
the Mediterranean Sea, is one
of the largest bivalve molluscs,
reaching a length of 60 cm (2 ft).

OPEN AND SHUT CASE
Although bivalves spend
much of their lives with
their valves slightly
apart, they must be
able to close the gap
quickly and securely to
protect themselves from
predators. For this
purpose, the two halves
of a bivalve shell match
perfectly and, when shut,
the opening can be just as
impenetrable as the
rest of the shell.

Cock's-comb
oyster

*Spine-covered
shell*

Fluted giant
clam

Baby noble pen shell

Spiny
sand cockle

MINIATURE PEOPLE-EATERS
There are many different types
and sizes of clams, but the biggest
of all shelled molluscs is the giant
clam, whose valves can measure
1.2 m (4 ft) and weigh over 250 kg
(0.25 ton). These huge shells have been put
to many uses by people, including bathtubs and
feeding troughs, and the shell is so strong that it
can be made into axe-heads with which to fell trees.
Living clams are said to have killed pearl divers by
trapping their arms or legs between the two valves.

Unusual partnerships

THERE ARE MANY TYPES of relationships in the animal world. A very familiar example is when one animal hunts and eats another. This is the predator–prey relationship, yet nature is not always so cut and thrust. On the seashore, as in other habitats, different kinds of animals are regularly seen together. In the relationship that is called parasitism, one partner, the parasite, gains, but the other, the host, loses. Some shore crabs are host to *Sacculina*, a strange creature related to the barnacles. *Sacculina* attaches itself to a young crab and then grows "tentacles" that eat into the crab's body, thus feeding itself and disabling the crab. In another type of relationship, called mutualism, both partners benefit. The hermit crab (*Pagurus bernhardus*) and the calliactis anemone (*Calliactis parasitica*) live in this way. The calliactis is sometimes called the parasitic anemone, but it does not seem to harm its hermit crab host. It feeds on particles that the crab drops, and the crab is protected by the anemone's stinging tentacles.

Hermit crab

Whelk shell

Calliactis anemone

THREE IN ONE
Each of the three animals in this group comes from a different major animal group. The hermit crab is a crustacean. The anemone is a coelenterate (pp. 72–73). The shell once belonged to a whelk, which is a sea-snail and member of the mollusc, or shellfish, group.

STING IN THE PINCER
The boxer crab carries small anemones in its pincers. They act as "stinging clubs" and are waved defensively at any creature that poses a threat to this very belligerent crustacean.

Anemone tentacles

Keelworm tubes inside shell

Claw of hermit crab

SWEEPING THE FLOOR
The tentacles of most anemones reach upwards for floating or swimming victims. A calliactis anemone on a hermit crab's shell tends to hang down and sweep the rocks for bits of food "spilt" by the hermit crab.

CLAW IN THE DOOR
In its defensive position, the hermit crab pulls itself deep inside the whelk shell. The right front claw (the cheliped), which bears the large pincer, is usually bigger than the left one, and the crab holds it across the shell's entrance to make an effective door, a barrier against predators.

OUT OF ITS SHELL

The hermit crab's soft, curled
abdomen is clearly visible when
the animal comes out of its shell.
When it grows too big for the
shell, it looks for another, larger
one. The two back pairs of legs
are small and adapted so the
hermit crab can hang on to
the inside of the shell.

*Artificial
whelk
shell*

HOME SWEET HOME

The hermit crab first makes
its home in smaller shells,
such as those of the topshell or
periwinkle, which the crab finds
on the seashore. When it grows
larger, the hermit crab usually lives in
whelk shells. Hermit crabs carry their
home around with them, and females of
the species carry eggs inside their shells
until they hatch. Then the larvae float in
the water with the rest of the plankton.

*Large pincer, or cheliped,
used to block entrance to
shell, providing extra security*

Antenna

SAFETY IN NUMBERS

Clown fish like
these tomato
clowns live
among the
stinging tentacles
of anemones. The
fish have special defences
in their body coverings to
prevent them from being stung.
It is thought that both partners
benefit from this arrangement in
various ways. The clown fish are safe in
the protective tentacles; they may drive off other fish that nibble at the anemone, and
they may eat leftover food caught by the anemone. The anemone may be "cleaned"
in the process and it may eat food dropped by the clown fish. It is also possible that
the colours of clown fish may warn predators, that the anemone is poisonous.

HOME IN A CONE

Not all hermit crabs live in whelk shells. This Pacific flat
hermit crab is occupying an empty omaria cone shell. The cone
shells are tropical molluscs; some species are extremely venomous.

Flower-like animals

OPEN FOR DINNER
Anemones are beautiful but deadly. The waving tentacles of a colony are a forest of danger for any small sea creatures that float or swim near them.

Scallop shell

ANEMONES ARE THE SURPRISING "flowers" of the shore – surprising because they are not flowers at all. They are hollow, jelly-like animals belonging to a group called the coelenterates or cnidarians, which also includes jellyfish and corals. Anemones are unable to move quickly so they cannot pursue prey or escape from predators. For them, the best form of attack and defence lies in their "petals" which are tentacles equipped with specialized stinging cells. Inside each cell is a capsule called a nematocyst which contains a long, coiled thread. In some species of anemone these are barbed, in others they contain venom. Stimulated by touch, or by particular chemicals, the threads flick out and either the barbs hold on to the prey, or venom is injected into it. The prey is pulled through the mouth into a digestive cavity where it is absorbed. Any remains are excreted through the mouth.

Mouth in centre of red beadlet anemone's body

TRAFFIC-LIGHT ANEMONES
Like flowers, anemones have evolved many beautiful colours even within the species. Beadlet anemones are found in various colours, including red, amber, and green. When the tide recedes, they fold in their tentacles and look like overgrown wine-gums scattered on the rocks. When fully grown, beadlet anemones have about 200 tentacles.

SWEEPING THE SEA
Fan worms are sometimes mistaken for anemones, but they belong to a different group of animals – the annelids (which include earthworms). The tentacles of the "fan" filter tiny food particles from the water and withdraw into the tube if danger threatens.

"FLOWER" ON A "STALK"
A side view of a beadlet anemone shows that it has a stubby "stalk" (body) with an iridescent sheen around the base. Beadlets can survive being out of water for some time, and can live quite high up on the shoreline.

A greyish beadlet anemone

FEATHERY PLUMES
The plumose, or frilled, anemone is brown, reddish, or white, and may grow up to 30 cm (1 ft) tall. Its feather tentacles catch very small bits of food and waft them down to the mouth by the beating action of tiny hairs called cilia.

*Snow-white tentacles
and brown body of a
beadlet anemone*

*Living cup coral
with tentacles
extended*

*Limy skeleton of
dead cup coral*

LIVING CORAL
Corals are similar to
anemones and members
of the same overall group,
the coelenterates. This cup
coral lives alone, unlike its (mostly)
tropical reef-building cousins.

MEDUSA OF THE SEAS
Snakelock anemones range
from grey with delicate sheens
or pink or green to all-over deep
green in colour. The tentacles, tipped
in deep pink, do not withdraw in this
species, even when it is out of water.

*The body "warts"
of this wartlet
anemone are
visible in this
closed-up
individual*

*Side view of dead
cup coral*

GIANT OF ITS KIND
The largest anemones may grow to
more than 1 m (3.3 ft) across. This
is a giant green anemone which
is found in tropical waters. It
can move, if only slowly,
sliding its muscular base
along the rock surface.

TINY GHOSTS
There are many species of
these tiny, ghost-white
encrusting anemones that
cover areas of rocky shore.
As the tide ebbs, most
anemones pull in their
tentacles and become
jelly-like blobs, to
avoid drying out.

*Encrusted remains
of barnacle shells*

*Acontia (strings)
of stinging cells*

*Coiled chalky
remains of
tube worm*

STINGING STRINGS
The colourful sagartia anemone
(this is the "rosea" variety) is one
of several species that eject pale,
stringy groups of stinging cells through
its mouth or through slits in its body
to defend itself or to catch a meal. The
"stings" are in fact parts of the animal's guts.

A fish in water

MOST FISH LIVE IN WATER, breathe by means of gills, swim and manoeuvre with fins, and are covered in an outer layer of transparent plates called scales. These scales vary in size and shape, but most are small and rounded, flexible, and single-layered. The skin underneath the scales produces a special mucus which makes the fish seem slimy and helps it glide easily through the water. All fish are vertebrates, that is they have a backbone and an internal skeleton. They use colour as a means of camouflage or defence, or to advertize a territory.

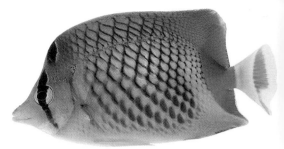

PEARLY SCALES
In the pearl-scaled butterfly fish, the yellow and orange colours, typical of butterfly fishes, are limited to the tail end. The large pearly scales give a rainbow effect of colour, and the fish's eye is camouflaged by a black stripe. The deep body but thin profile of the butterfly fish means that it can slip easily between pieces of coral and plant stems.

Tall dorsal fin

Stout spines on back

Yellow dorsal fin of ribbon eel

Large, gaping mouth

Pectoral fin

Flat back because fish hangs just below surface waiting for flies

Silver hatchetfish
Argyropelecus lychnus

FRESHWATER COUSIN
The silver hatchetfish, with its extraordinary deep belly, can leap from the water, while beating its large pectoral fins, and "fly" short distances, skimming the surface of the water. This is a freshwater fish found in South America; a different type of hatchetfish lives in the deep sea.

HUNGRY PREDATOR
The European John Dory is deep-bodied but extremely thin. It creeps up on smaller fish and prawns, keeping head on to make itself look inconspicuous. Then its great jaws suddenly lever forward and engulf the prey. The John Dory is well protected by the sets of stout spines in front of its dorsal and anal fins.

European John Dory
Zeus faber

IN SHOALS
Young cod feed at the surface on small crustaceans. The adults feed in deeper water on small fish, crustaceans, and worms. They swim in a shoal, so it is hard for predators to catch them.

Colours protect fish in a variety of
ways. Smooth and silvery greens, blues, and
browns camouflage some species, such as this
wrasse in open water. A riot of brilliant reds,
yellows, and blues conceal others on a coral reef.
Spots, stripes, and patches disrupt a fish's
normal outline and confuse predators.

Corkwing wrasse
Crenilabrus melops

Ribbon eel

*Skin is
slimy and
slippery*

*Ribbon eel is
more like a snake
than a fish*

SNAKE OF THE SEA
There are about 600 species of
true eels, including freshwater eels,
congers, morays, pike eels, and gulpers.
The gaily-coloured ribbon eel is a type of
moray. Like its cousins, it lurks in cracks
and caves, waiting for prey to pass
nearby. It then seizes the victim
with a fast, snake-like strike
of the head and a snap of
the sharp-toothed jaws.
The ribbon eel can coil
itself backwards into
crevices that seem
far too small for
its long, thin body.

*Sensory
barbels*

Large pectoral fins

WALKING FISH
The tub gurnard uses the
spiny rays of its pectoral fins to creep
delicately along the sea bottom. The first
three rays of each pectoral fin are separate
and move to and fro like spider's legs. The
enormous size of its pectoral fins and its spiny fin
rays make the tub gurnard an extremely prickly fish.

Tub gurnard
Trigla lucerna

Moving along

FLYING FISH
Gathering speed underwater, flying fish leap clear of the surface to escape predators. They can then glide for over 30 seconds by spreading out the side fins.

AT SCHOOL
Fish often swim together in a school like these blue-striped snappers. In schools, a single fish is less likely to be attacked by a predator than if it was swimming on its own. The moving mass of individuals may confuse the predator, and there are more pairs of eyes on the lookout.

EVERY SWIMMER KNOWS that it is harder to move an arm or a leg through seawater than through air. To be a fast swimmer like a dolphin, tuna, or sailfish, it helps to have a shape which is streamlined like a torpedo to reduce drag (resistance to water). A smooth skin and few projections from the body allow an animal to move through the water more easily. The density of seawater has an advantage in that it helps to support the weight of very heavy bodies, even the heaviest animal that ever lived on earth, the blue whale, which weighs up to 150 tonnes (147.6 tons). Some heavy-shelled creatures, like the chambered nautilus, have gas-filled floats to stop them from sinking. Some ocean animals, such as dolphins and flying fish, get up enough speed underwater to leap briefly into the air, but not all ocean animals are good swimmers. Many can only swim slowly, some drift along in the currents, crawl along the bottom, burrow in the sand, or stay put, anchored to the seabed.

IN THE SWING
During the day, many electric rays prefer to stay hidden on the sandy bottom, relying on their electric organs for defence, but they do swim if disturbed and at night when searching for prey. There are more than 30 kinds of electric ray, mostly living in warm waters. Most other rays have spindly tails (unlike the electric ray's broad tail), and move through water using their pectoral fins. Waves pass from the front to the back of the pectoral fins, which, in larger rays like mantas, become so exaggerated that the fins actually beat up and down.

Spiracle (a one-way valve) takes in water, which is pumped out through gill slits

Electric ray's smooth skin can be either dark green or brown in colour

Electric rays can grow to 1.8 m (6 ft) and weigh as much as 50 kg (110 lb)

Pelvic fin

DIVING DEEP
True seals move through water by beating their back flippers and tail from side to side and using their front flippers to steer. Their nostrils are closed to prevent water entering the airways. Harbour seals (right) can dive up to 600 m (2,000 ft). Seals do not suffer from the bends, because they breathe out before diving and, unlike humans, do not breathe compressed air. When underwater, seals use oxygen which is stored in their blood.

Broad tail fin, swinging from side to side, helps propel ray along

Pectoral fin provides extra propulsion as waves pass along flexible edges of its rounded side

Smaller second dorsal fin

Clasper (male reproductive organ)

Swimming sequence of an electric ray
Torpedo nobiliana

Electric organ, at base of pectoral fin, helps catch fish by stunning them – some species can deliver over 200 volts

Model of great white shark
Carcharodon carcharias

TAKING OFF
Dolphins leap out of water for fun, in order to signal to other dolphins, and when feeding. They can also porpoise (skim over the water for short distances) when moving at speed. They can do this because it is easier to move in air, which puts less friction on their bodies.

Tall dorsal fin

Pectoral fin

Pelvic fin

Tail propels shark forward in water

Starry smooth-hound
Mustelus asterias

Undulations (S-shaped waves) pass down body, ending at the tail which produces forward thrust

LEAN MACHINE
Sharks propel themselves through the water by beating their tails from side to side. The pectoral fins are held out from the body and as water flows over them, the fins act like aeroplanes' wings and keep the shark from sinking. When the fins are tilted they also act as brakes, just like the flaps on the wings of an aeroplane which are raised on landing. Some sharks that live on the seabed, such as horn sharks and epaulette sharks, can use their pectoral fins to crawl along the bottom.

Mobile molluscs

MOLLUSCS ARE A LARGE GROUP of animals that includes cephalopods (octopuses, squid, and cuttlefish), bivalves (scallops, mussels, and oysters), and gastropods (snails, limpets, and abalones). Cephalopods have a small shell or no shell, and a muscular body wall that can expel water, so they can move by jet propulsion. Bivalves have a shell that is in two halves, and some, such as scallops, also swim using jet propulsion. Most clams, however, can only bury themselves in the sand, or are anchored to the seabed. Gastropods usually have a coiled external shell, although some, such as slugs, have a small internal shell or no shell at all. They travel along a surface by moving the muscles of their single flat foot.

INK SCREEN
Cephalopods like this squid produce a cloud of ink when threatened. This confuses an enemy and allows time for the squid to escape. The ink is produced in a gland linked to the gut and is ejected in a blast of water from the tubelike funnel near its head.

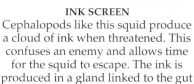

MOVING LIKE A SNAIL
Great pond snails move slowly, on a single, large, flat foot, among water plants looking for food. The muscles of the foot move in and out in waves, and as each wave passes along the foot, the snail moves forwards. Special glands produce a slime that helps the foot glide smoothly along.

JET PROPULSION
Squid are very efficient at swimming by jet propulsion. Their torpedo-shaped bodies are permanently streamlined so that they can swim fast to escape predators, and it may be no coincidence that they are among the most common animals living in the ocean.

Squid
Loligo forbisi

Eye with horizontal iris

Tentacle, also known as "leg" or "arm"

Funnel, or siphon through which octopus squeezes water when swimming

Two rows of suckers under each tentacle

Powerful suckers grip rocky surfaces, so octopus can pull itself along, or hold prey

Common octopus
Octopus vulgaris

Tentacles trail out behind body when octopus takes off

Body streamlined to reduce drag (resistance to water)

Eye is similar to human eye and used to spot prey

Lesser octopus
Eledone cirrhosa

3 FAST RETREAT
If threatened, the octopus jets off. It can move very quickly by taking water into its body cavity and forcing it out again through its funnel, so pushing the octopus along. Octopuses can eject a cloud of ink in the same way if attacked. They dart away under cover of the ink cloud and immediately change colour to confuse their pursuer.

Visceral hump contains mantle muscles and vital organs, and stomach

2 IN THE SWIM
If possible, an octopus keeps one leg fixed to a rocky surface, so that it can rapidly pull itself down to the seabed if it needs to hide. To move slowly off the bottom, the octopus squirts water gently out of a funnel that sticks out from the edge of its baglike body. However, when it needs to travel at speed, the octopus moves with its arms trailing behind.

Water jet near hinge propels scallop forward

1 ON THE BOTTOM
The common octopus hides during the day in a rocky lair, emerging at night to look for crabs and crustaceans. It "walks" slowly over the rocky surface, using its eight tentacles in a similar manner to the way a human uses legs. When it is close enough, it pounces on the prey.

Scallop shell is made of two halves called valves

Muscular mantle (below skin of head) that pushes water out through funnel when swimming

Sensory tentacles

IN THE SWIM
Scallops launch themselves off the bottom by squeezing water out of the back of their shells either side of the hinge. Schools of scallops may take off and swim together. If a predator approaches, such as a starfish, the scallop shoots a jet of water out of the front of the shell and zips off hinge first.

The importance of water

WATER IS AN ESSENTIAL PART of an amphibian's (the word means "double life") existence. Amphibians need fresh water to keep their skin moist, and most species need a watery environment to reproduce – especially species that spend all, or part, of their lives as larvae under water. In aquatic or watery habitats, water passes rapidly through the skin and has to be eliminated via the kidneys. In dry areas, amphibians risk losing more water than they can take up. Frogs can reduce water loss by having a less porous skin, by seeking out damp, shady places, by burrowing, and by taking up water from damp or wet surfaces. Some toads obtain almost three-quarters of the water they need through a baggy patch or "seat" on their pelvis which they press against moist surfaces. Amphibians rarely drink water, although a little may be taken in with food. They have adapted their behaviour and skin-surface structure to a variety of habitats. They live in ponds and trees, and high in the forest canopy where the only free-standing water collects in pockets formed by leaves. They have also adapted to life in the desert, by burrowing and forming cocoons.

FLOWER POWER
Amphibians frequently feature in fiction. *Thumbelina* is a children's story about a flower fairy stolen by a toad who wants her to marry his ugly son. The old toad imprisons Thumbelina on a lily pad in the middle of a river, but helped by the fishes, she escapes and eventually marries the Prince of the Flower People.

Female great crested newt
Triturus cristatus

Young tiger salamander,
Ambystoma tigrinum,
with gills

BREATHING UNDERWATER
The larva of the tiger salamander uses its three pairs of large, feathery gills to breathe under water. The deep red gills are rich in blood vessels, which absorb the dissolved air from the water.

WET AND DRY
Great crested newts spend most of the year on land, returning to the water to breed in spring. Once in the water they shed their dry, warty skin to reveal a new, smoother one.

One of three pairs of gills

Sequence of Australian water-holding frog, *Cyclorana platycephalus*, burrowing

A CAVE SALAMANDER
The cave-dwelling olm lives in cold, underground streams along the Adriatic coast of Italy and Croatia. It is a sexually mature larva like the axolotl (see below), but, unlike the axolotl, it will not become an adult if iodine is added to the water, or if it is given hormone treatment.

Olm, *Proteus anguinus*, ranges in length from 20–30 cm (8–12 in)

1 BURROWING
Like many other amphibians the Australian water-holding frog burrows into the ground to avoid drying out. In an underground chamber, the frog survives long droughts in desert conditions.

LIFE AND ART
Frogs are often used in ornaments and designs, like this frog-shaped flagon, made in China during the 16th century.

Flagon used to hold water

2 STAYING UNDERGROUND
In the underground chamber, the moisture level is higher and the surrounding temperature is lower than outside. The frog also stores water in its bladder.

3 COMING UP FOR AIR
The frog sheds the outer layers of its skin to form a cocoon, reducing water loss. The frog emerges to feed and breed only when the rains come.

Adult lives on dry land in leaf litter or small burrows

California newt, *Taricha torosa*, ranges in length from 13–20 cm (5–8 in)

Powerful back leg

Full webbing on foot

Albino African clawed toad *Xenopus larvis*

AN UNDERWATER LIFE
The African clawed toad spends most of its life in water, only coming on to land to migrate to nearby ponds or lakes where it spawns. The flattened head and body, powerful back legs, and webbed feet make this toad an excellent swimmer.

CALIFORNIA NEWT
This newt lays a round clump of 12–24 eggs on underwater plants in late winter to early spring. The young newts leave the water the following autumn or early spring.

Flat body

Feathery red gills

Axolotl
Ambystoma mexicanus

WATER BABY
In some species of newt and salamander, larvae never develop into adults. Instead they remain in the water and become sexually mature in the larval state. This is known as "neoteny". Neoteny may be caused by something in the environment, such as low water temperature, or a low level of iodine in the water. The axolotl (left) is the best known example of a neotenous larva.

On all fours

NEWTS AND SALAMANDERS usually move quite slowly. They walk or crawl – on land, underground, in the trees, or on the bottom of ponds – but they will move quickly to escape danger. Some salamanders live among grasses, on low bushes, and even high up in the trees; they have stubby, webbed feet for gripping leaves. Certain species can also burrow or swim: the mole and tiger salamanders burrow with their hands and feet, and the male aquatic newt performs a swimming courtship display in front of the female. In this, they are similar to another relatively unknown group of amphibians – the worm-like and legless caecilians. Most of the 170 species of caecilians are burrowers, but one group actually lives in water.

SWIMMING NEWT
Swimming involves many different leg, body, and tail movements. Newts float with legs outstretched and body slightly inflated with air. Slow, lazy, swimming movements are made, using the legs like oars in a two-person rowing boat. To move faster, they paddle with the front legs alone, with the hind legs, or sometimes with both together.

Japanese fire-bellied newt

Foot in forward position ready for next step

Tail is straight

Foot presses against ground, pushing body forward

Foot pushes body forward

Tail curves to right, helping salamander to balance

Foot in forward position ready to press against ground and push forward

Foot moves forward

Front foot pushes body forward

1 ONWARD AND UPWARD
The European fire salamander walks slowly like most salamanders. The legs move in an alternate and opposite pattern, which means that the salamander lifts and moves the front foot of one side forward at the same time as the hind foot on the other side of its body. The other two feet remain in the same position on the ground, pushing the body forward, ready for the next step in the sequence.

*Foot ready to lift
for next step*

*Foot about
to push body
forward*

*Foot
ready to
push body
forward*

3 FORWARD MARCH

The third step completes the sequence, with the left front and right hind feet together and the other two feet stationary. As well as pushing the salamander forward, this alternate and opposite walking pattern pushes the middle of its body from side to side. The swaying motion increases with walking speed and looks like a baby crawling.

*Foot about to
lift and move
forward*

*Foot ready to lift
and move forward*

*Foot in
forward
position*

UNDULATING CAECILIANS

Most caecilians live in soft earth or in the leaf litter of the tropical rainforest floor. About 20 species have moved back into the water and swim using undulating, or wave-like, movements like the one above. All caecilians can burrow, pushing their head into the soil, and opening up a hole with movements of the neck. Then they either "swim" forward through the soil with undulating movements that pass back along the body, or use a special, worm-like concertina movement, where the spine folds inside the body.

2 NEXT STEP

With the next step the front right and left hind feet of the salamander move together, while the other two feet stay in the same position on the ground, getting ready to push the body forward.

*Foot pressing on
surface, ready to
push body forward*

*Foot about
to lift*

*Foot ready to
lift and move
body forward*

NEWT WALK

When on land and moving at slow speed, newts walk in a similar way to salamanders. This view from beneath shows which foot is actively pressing against the surface, pushing the newt forward, and which is being lifted off the surface before being put down again. When in water, the newt is lighter and more buoyant (just as a person is in a swimming-pool) and often uses just the tips of its fingers and toes to walk over the muddy bottom of its pond.

*Foot
pressing down*

View from below of a
newt walking

*Foot
ready
to lift
and move
body forward*

A tight squeeze

ALL SNAKES EAT MEAT, and they have had to develop many different ways of killing their food. Some kill their prey with venom, but boas and pythons feed mainly on mammals, which they kill by constriction. Constrictors do not crush their victims as many people think. The snake coils its body around its struggling victim, making it harder and harder for the prey to breathe, until it finally suffocates. The snake applies just enough pressure to match the breathing movements of the prey. Any mammal from a mouse to a deer could be that prey, depending on the size of the snake. In fact, giant snakes can swallow surprisingly large animals. An anaconda over 8 m (26 ft) long can eat a caiman 2 m (6.5 ft) long, although it may take more than a week to digest the meal.

TO THE RESCUE!
There are only a few Asian and African records of humans who have been killed and eaten by some of the larger species of pythons. In one of the famous Tintin books, Zorrino the guide has a lucky escape (contrary to appearances), saved just in the nick of time by his friend, the redoubtable Tintin.

DANGEROUS ACT
Music hall and circus act performers who dance with constrictors are taking a great risk. This dancer was nearly suffocated by a python, and was rescued only seconds before certain death.

2 DEADLY EMBRACE
The constricting snake reacts to every tiny movement of the rat, tightening its grip all the time. It responds to even the smallest vibrations produced by the rat's beating heart, and the snake will not release its hold until the beating finally stops. Death is fairly quick and bones are rarely broken. The snake then shifts the rat so that it can be swallowed head-first.

3 BIG MOUTH
The snake's mouth is very flexible. The jaws move easily together from side to side, while the backward-pointing teeth grip tightly. As the powerful jaws move over the head of the rat, it looks as though the snake is "walking over" its food.

4 SAFETY FIRST
It may take only one or two gulps before a small animal disappears completely, but it takes an hour or more for some of the larger victims. The amazing swallowing action of the snake is mainly automatic, and the prey is drawn in by the trunk muscles of the snake. If, however, the snake is frightened or disturbed while it is eating prey, it is able to regurgitate its meal in order to escape.

Body can expand to allow for large prey

5 TIGHT FIT
Most of the rat has now disappeared. The flexible ligament, rather like an elastic muscle that connects the two halves of the snake's lower jaw, allows the snake to open its mouth very wide. As the lower jaws are forced apart, the muscle between them stretches to the shape of the prey.

Dinner time

If a meal walks by that might put up a fight, a snake can usually afford to ignore it. After an enormous feast, when a constrictor, might work its way through an entire leopard, the snake may not eat again for as much as a year.

1 FANGS OF DEATH
When a boa constrictor attacks prey, it has to find somewhere it can start swallowing, usually at the head. If the victim is wriggly, like this rat, the snake strikes with its long, front teeth. The rat secure in its jaws, the boa starts to coil round it.

Prey is swallowed head-first so that it cannot attack the snake

Special hinged bone

Jaw closed

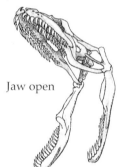
Jaw open

OPEN WIDE
The jaws of a snake are very flexible, so its prey can be swallowed headfirst and whole, even when the victim's body is wider than the snake's. A special bone, linking the lower jaw to the skull, works like a double-jointed hinge. The lower jaw can be stretched sideways because the two halves are connected at the chin by a flexible ligament that works like an elastic muscle.

SNAKE EATS SNAKE
When a California king snake meets a rattlesnake, it grips the rattler with its jaws just behind the head. Then the king snake loops its body around the victim, squeezing until the rattler suffocates.

WILD CAT STRIKE
In Kenya, a Thompson's gazelle falls victim to a cheetah. The massive jaws of the cat clamp on to the throat of the struggling prey, probably causing it to suffocate in the same way as a boa suffocates its prey. It is probably finished off by the sharp teeth and claws of the cheetah.

Rat's tail

6 END OF THE ROAD
At this point the snake could be faced with breathing problems, but it overcomes them by pushing its windpipe forward towards the front of its mouth, using the windpipe as a built-in "snorkel".

Lizards

THERE ARE OVER 3,000 species of lizard. They form the most successful of all the reptilian groups, having evolved many different lifestyles. Although most of them live on the ground, many live in trees, some are burrowers, and some are aquatic. Some lizards have no limbs and are snake-like; others can parachute or fly. The lizards on these two pages all live in desert regions, where they are more numerous than snakes. They like to bask in the sun in the early morning to warm up their muscles after a cold desert night. In the heat of the day, they retreat into the shade of rocks or plants, down cool burrows, or even clamber into bushes. Most desert lizards change colour to blend into their backgrounds and avoid being spotted by predators. When threatened, some lizards put on intimidating displays. If this does not work, then some lizards will bite, but most simply run away.

FIERCE FRILLS
The frilled lizard of the Australian desert spreads out the frill around its neck to make itself look larger to scare away enemies. The frill is supported by rods, just like those of an umbrella, which are attached to a bone at the base of the tongue.

Fringe of scales on toe

FRINGE TOES
This fast-moving lizard can run across the sand dunes in the Sahara, where it lives. It has a fringe of scales on its feet which act like snowshoes to spread its weight so that it does not sink into the sand. To stay cooler on hot sand, it holds its head and body high above the surface of the ground.

Tail and opposing toes grip plants as chameleon climbs

CHAMELEON
A chameleon sits on the stem of a welwitschia plant growing in the Namib Desert. Chameleons and other lizards are attracted to the plant because insects like to shelter under the shade of its leaves. They catch the insects by shooting out their long, sticky-tipped tongues.

GILA MONSTER
The Gila monster is one of only two lizards with a venomous bite, although it is seldom fatal to humans. Gila monsters live in desert scrub and are mainly active at night, feeding on small mammals, snakes, and other lizards.

Layer of skin under the scales changes colour for camouflage

Bearded dragon

Beard not apparent when lizard at rest

In places, the scales form spines

Colour darker in morning to absorb heat of the sun, and paler as day wears on

BEARDED DRAGON
A formidable-looking lizard, the bearded dragon from the dry interior of Australia has spiny skin to protect itself from predators. The beard under the chin expands to make the dragon look even more impressive. Bearded dragons feed on insects, birds' eggs, newborn small mammals, and some dew soaked plants. They are active in the early morning and late afternoon, climbing into shrubs where it is cooler at midday.

Sturdy tail serves as a fat reserve

LIZARD EGGS
These eggs belong to the eyed lizard from northern Africa. They lay up to 20 eggs in sandy soil and these hatch out two to three months later. Eyed lizards reach over 60 cm (2 ft) long. These large lizards feed on insects, small mammals, and other reptiles.

SPINY-TAILED OR DAB LIZARD
One of the hardiest desert lizards in the Sahara, the African spiny-tailed lizard tolerates high temperatures and survives on small amounts of water from dew and on the plants and few insects that it eats. This lizard is active in the day but avoids the midday heat by staying in its deep burrow.

THORNY DEVIL
A spiny body helps to protect this lizard from being attacked. It lives in deserts in Australia, and has a similar ant-eating lifestyle to horned toads. Thorny devils collect rain or dew on their backs, which finds its way down tiny channels into their mouths. These lizards are also known as molochs.

Keen sense of smell helps lizard hunt

Collared lizard
Crotaphytus collaris

Wide gape to deter predators

Sharp teeth can inflict nasty bite

COLLARED LIZARD
In a defensive pose, the collared lizard opens its mouth in a wide gape. If molested, the lizard will bite. In preference to biting an attacker it will leap away over the rocks where it lives in the deserts of the southwestern United States. The collared lizard is an active predator. It hunts during the day for insects, smaller lizards, and small snakes and mice. Highly agile, it can even leap into the air to catch flying insects.

Long claws for gripping rocks

Birds of a feather

THERE ARE OVER 9,000 species of birds in the world – flying and flightless, brightly coloured and dull-hued, huge like the ostrich or tiny like the hummingbirds. Birds are the only creatures to have feathers, and these are lightweight, strong, and flexible. Birds also have two wings, a strong bill, no teeth, scaly legs and feet, and three or four toes with claws on the end. Like mammals, birds breathe air, have a skeleton and are warm-blooded. Unlike most mammals, they lay eggs. Bird colours help individuals of the same species identify each other, and they also help birds attract a mate, threaten a rival, or camouflage themselves.

WADER
The black crake of east Africa has long, widely spaced toes to stop it sinking into the mud and to help it walk over floating water plants. The short, thick bill is used to peck small invertebrates and seeds off the surface of the water.

FLIGHTLESS
The brown kiwi, *Apteryx Australis*, is a medium-sized flightless bird that lives in New Zealand. It is nocturnal and eats worms, beetles, grubs, and berries which it finds by smelling with the nostrils at the end of its long bill.

Zebra finch
Taeniopygia guttata

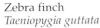

Short, seed-eating bill

Distinctive stripes round bill

SEED-EATER
The colourful zebra finch lives on the dry grasslands of Australia, where it is one of the most common birds. Pairs of these gregarious birds mate for life, living in flocks of between 10 and 100 birds, and breeding within the group. In the drier areas, they lay eggs whenever it is warm enough and there is enough rain to sustain their young. Zebra finches are perching birds as well as strong fliers. They feed on grass seeds and insects and are well known as songbirds.

Mandarin duck
Aix galericulata

Female

Short legs set well back on body

Male

Powerful grip for perching

WATERBIRD
Mandarin ducks live near ponds and lakes surrounded by woods, where they nest in tree holes. Like so many other bird species, the male is more colourful than the female. However, both male and female moult their feathers and the male is as drab-coloured as the female – until his new feathers grow. Ducks have webbed feet and broad, flat bills.

DIVING BIRD

Great white pelicans live in swamps and marshes, and usually fish in groups, making a circle and herding the fish together to scoop them up. A pelican's bill can hold more food than its stomach, and the bird has a daily intake of 1 kg (over 2 lb). Pelicans can hold prey in their throat pouch in order to transport it back to their nest.

Great white pelican
Pelecanus onocrotabus

Throat pouch

Large, webbed feet

Powerful hooked bill used to tear prey into bite-sized pieces

Golden eagle
Aquila chrysaetos

BIRD OF PREY

Like all other birds of prey, the golden eagle uses its talons to catch and carry prey, and its sharp, hooked bill to pull apart the animals it kills. It hunts for medium-sized mammals and birds, and will scavenge on carcasses as well. It is a very good flier, and the most numerous large eagle in the northern hemisphere. It makes its nest, or eyrie, out of branches on high crags and rocky places. The eagle is named after the golden feathers on the top of the head and the back of the neck.

Broad, rounded wings

Golden eagles can be 104 cm (41 in) tall

Sharp talons to hold prey

Primary flight feathers, used for power and steering

Bats prefer to hang upside down using a five-clawed grip

Unlike some bats, fruit bat is tailless

Thin, muscular wing membrane

Large, forward-facing eyes

Keen sense of smell

Male and female bats call to each other during the breeding season

Coarse fur typical of mammals

Lighter coloured ring of fur around neck

Upper arm

Forearm outstretched in flight

Blood vessels seen through wing membrane

A FURRY FLYING FRUIT-EATER

This male Borneo fruit bat has a fox-like face which explains why some fruit bats are nicknamed "flying foxes". These bats tend to use their excellent eyesight and keen sense of smell rather than echo-location to hunt for their prey. At dusk they fly from their roosts to feed, and in farming areas they can do enormous damage to crops. However, they are also an essential part of the local ecosystem, since they transfer pollen from plant to plant as they feed and disperse plant seeds in their droppings. The fruit they feed on is not necessarily eaten whole. Some bats work it around their mouth, moving it from cheek to cheek, biting and sucking loudly and eventually swallowing only the juices. The left-over fibres and chewed-up fruit husks are then spat on to the ground below. It is not a pleasant experience to be beneath a flock of these hungry creatures when they are feeding.

Fliers in the night

BATS ARE UNIQUE in that they are the only mammals that can fly. They are second only to rodents as the most numerous species – there are about 950 different kinds. Bats vary enormously in size, ranging from the tiny hog-nosed bat which measures just 13 cm (5 in) with its wings outstetched, to the large flying fox which is the size of a small dog and has a wingspan of 2 m (6.5 ft). Bats' wings are made of thin sheets of muscle and elastic fibres covered by skin. The bones of the arm and the second to fifth fingers support the wing; the first finger or "thumb" sticks out like a claw and may be used to crawl, groom, fight, or hold food. In flight, some bats can reach speeds of more than 50 km/h (30 mph). Their wings are powered by the same muscles as a human uses to "flap" his arms, but the muscles are much stronger in proportion to the size of a bat's body. Bats are one of the most sociable groups of mammals. They roost together in their thousands in caves or trees and some species help each other in the nightly hunt for food.

PEGASUS
People have always been fascinated by the possibility of flight. Observation of animals such as bats has led to the invention of many fanciful creatures, including the mythical flying horse, Pegasus.

5th finger
4th finger
3rd finger
2nd finger
1st finger

OTHER FLIERS
Although bats are the only mammals capable of flight with wings, other mammals such as possums, flying squirrels, and flying lemurs can glide on the air. They use a membrane which acts as a kind of parachute.

MOTHER AND CHILD
A baby bat clings to its mother's furry abdomen and suckles milk, just like any other mammal.

FROM MOTHS TO BUDS TO BLOOD
Most bats are insectivores, eating moths, midges, flies, and other nocturnal insects. This fruit bat feeds on buds and the soft parts of plants. Vampire bats bite mammals and birds to drink their blood, but do not usually attack humans.

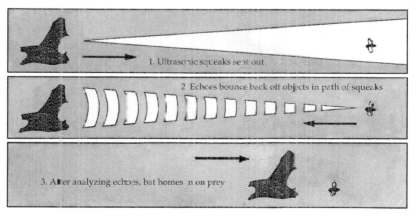

1. Ultrasonic squeaks sent out

2. Echoes bounce back off objects in path of squeaks

3. After analyzing echoes, bat homes in on prey

"SEEING" WITH SOUND
Bats hear in the dark, using what is known as echo-location. Their mouth sends out high-pitched squeaks (1). The sound waves bounce off anything in their path and return to the bat's ears as echoes (2). The bat's brain analyzes the pattern of echoes to form a "sound picture" with which it can locate and home in on its prey (3).

FUNCTIONAL FACES
The curved flaps on the noses of horseshoe bats and leaf-nosed bats help with echo-location. A long, hairy tongue is useful for catching insects.

Horseshoe bat   Leaf-nosed bat   Bat with hair-fringed tongue

Rodent success

RODENTS ARE GREAT survivors. They have the ability to adapt to changing circumstances or their environment, and are very good at protecting or defending themselves. Rodents make up the order Rodentia, which is the largest order of mammals, with more than 1,700 species, including squirrels, chipmunks, rats, beavers, and gerbils. Rodents usually have two incisors in each jaw, short forelimbs for manipulating food, and cheek pouches for storing food. Like other mammals, rodents have furry coats to keep them warm and dry, and they groom themselves or each other regularly to get rid of parasites and dirt. Many rodents live underground in burrows, because there the temperatures do not fluctuate as much as they do on the surface. Desert rodents such as the pallid gerbil escape the extreme heat of the desert day in a cool burrow, and during the cold desert nights, find that the burrow is warmer than outside.

Pallid gerbils have long tail for balance while leaping and running

Chinchilla
Chinchilla laniger

HUNGRY CHINCHILLA
Chinchillas eat nuts, just like the chipmunk below, by turning them over and over in their paws as they nibble. These luxuriously coated creatures live in the high, rocky mountains of South America, where they spend much time and energy grooming their long, thick fur so it will protect them efficiently from the bitter mountain cold and wind.

Shaw's jird
Meriones meridianus

Tail helps jird balance on hind legs

BALANCING ACT
Jirds are related to gerbils and together they are the largest groups of small mammals living in the dry regions of Africa and Asia. This large jird, its body measuring up to 20 cm (8 in) long, lives in Morocco, Algeria, Tunisia, and Egypt. They are adept at leaping and climbing and balance easily on their hind legs.

Chipmunk
Tamius striatus

Nut is rotated in manipulative forepaws

Distinctive stripes in fur on back

Strong back paws for climbing

Short, fluffy tail

HAND TO MOUTH
The chipmunk holding food in its hand-like forepaws is a common sight in eastern North America. These naturally curious members of the squirrel family frequent picnic sites and parks in the hope of finding leftover titbits. The chipmunk manipulates food in a very efficient way. As it feeds, it rotates the nut quickly, scraping off loose bits, and testing with its teeth to find the weak point where the nut can be cracked. Like many other rodents, it carries surplus food in cheek pouches back to the burrow.

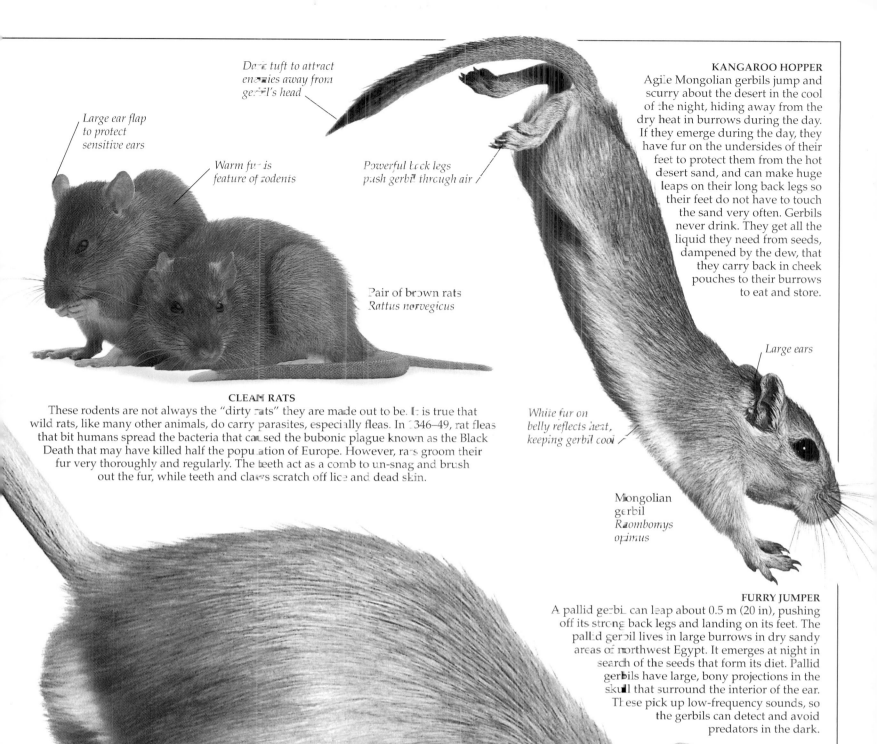

Dark tuft to attract enemies away from gerbil's head

Large ear flap to protect sensitive ears

Warm fur is feature of rodents

Powerful back legs push gerbil through air

Pair of brown rats
Rattus norvegicus

KANGAROO HOPPER

Agile Mongolian gerbils jump and scurry about the desert in the cool of the night, hiding away from the dry heat in burrows during the day. If they emerge during the day, they have fur on the undersides of their feet to protect them from the hot desert sand, and can make huge leaps on their long back legs so their feet do not have to touch the sand very often. Gerbils never drink. They get all the liquid they need from seeds, dampened by the dew, that they carry back in cheek pouches to their burrows to eat and store.

Large ears

White fur on belly reflects heat, keeping gerbil cool

Mongolian gerbil
Rhombomys opimus

CLEAN RATS

These rodents are not always the "dirty rats" they are made out to be. It is true that wild rats, like many other animals, do carry parasites, especially fleas. In 1346–49, rat fleas that bit humans spread the bacteria that caused the bubonic plague known as the Black Death that may have killed half the population of Europe. However, rats groom their fur very thoroughly and regularly. The teeth act as a comb to un-snag and brush out the fur, while teeth and claws scratch off lice and dead skin.

FURRY JUMPER

A pallid gerbil can leap about 0.5 m (20 in), pushing off its strong back legs and landing on its feet. The pallid gerbil lives in large burrows in dry sandy areas of northwest Egypt. It emerges at night in search of the seeds that form its diet. Pallid gerbils have large, bony projections in the skull that surround the interior of the ear. These pick up low-frequency sounds, so the gerbils can detect and avoid predators in the dark.

Big ears to pick up sounds of nearby danger

Unusually long back legs for jumping

Eyes give wide field of view

Pallid gerbil family Gerbillinae

King of the Arctic

IN EVERY HABITAT there is a dominant predator, and the polar bear is the largest and most powerful hunter of the Arctic. There are probably 20,000 polar bears wandering over the vast Arctic ice floes, some of them even roaming as far as the North Pole. Polar bears are solitary animals except in the breeding season. They do not hibernate, and in the long winter, when the Arctic pack ice extends farther out to sea, they hunt for seals beneath the ice. Their small ears help to prevent heat loss, and they have a third eyelid, like a cat, which protects the eyes from snow blindness. Their dense fur keeps them warm even when the temperature drops to −58°C (−72°F). An undercoat of thick fur is protected by an outer coat of long guard hairs. These hairs stick together when they get wet, forming a waterproof barrier. Under the fur, a thick layer of blubber performs two roles, insulating the bear against the cold, and acting as a food store, to help the bear survive hard times.

Polar bear
Tharlactos maritimus

Small, rounded ears help prevent heat loss

HEAVYWEIGHT
Polar bears are twice the size of a tiger – an average adult male polar bear measuring 2.5 m (8 ft) from head to tail and weighing over 500 kg (1,100 lb). Female polar bears are much smaller than the males, measuring 2 m (6.5 ft) and weighing over 320 kg (705 lb). To maintain this size, polar bears sometimes eat as much 68 kg (150 lbs) of seal blubber and entrails in one sitting. After they have fed, they lick their fur and wipe their face with a paw, very like a cat.

Polar bears rely on scent and light reflected from the snow to guide them

Air vent scraped in roof lets stale air escape

GARBAGE DISPOSAL
When polar bears find it hard to hunt live food such as seals, they become omnivorous, and are often attracted by human waste products. The rubbish dumps on the edge of Churchill in Canada are a favourite haunt for these enormous animals.

BEAR JOURNEYS
In their quest for food, polar bears make long journeys across the Arctic. In fact, they spend most of their lives walking on pack ice in a world of twilight and darkness. They are expert divers and swimmers, and often hitch rides on ice floes – one was even found swimming 320 km (190 miles) from land. They also dive from the top of icebergs more than 15 m (50 ft) into the water.

CAVE CUBS
Polar bear cubs are born in December or January in a warm, cosy den dug in the snow by the mother. The cubs – usually two of them, but sometimes one or three – grow rapidly on their mother's rich milk, which is about 30 per cent fat. While in the ice cave, the mother has nothing to eat and lives on the stored fat in her body.

POLAR PADDLE
Polar bears are slow, but very strong and efficient swimmers underwater, and able to keep going for a long time. They use only their front legs to propel themselves; the back legs are held still and used to steer the body like a rudder.

FAVOURITE FOOD
Over 90 per cent of a polar bear's diet consists of seals. They wait by a seal's blowhole in the ice, pouncing as soon as the seal comes up for air. One stroke of the bear's massive paw and a bite at the back of the skull kills the seal. But most hunting trips are unsuccessful, and a bear may not eat for up to five days.

Yellow-white fur acts as camouflage

Powerful legs to outrun prey

Hollow hairs trap warm air near body

Thickly padded soles covered by rough skin and sometimes tough hair

Sharp claws for grabbing prey

Non-slip soles help grip slippery ice

Living in a troop

WESTERN LOWLAND GORILLAS (*Gorilla gorilla gorilla*) live
in tropical rainforests in central Africa. A gorilla troop is
usually made up of about 5 to 15 animals. The leader of the
group is an adult male called a silverback because of his
colouring. Apart from the silverback, the troop may
include one or two young adult males, several adult
females, and a number of juveniles and infants. The
gorillas are fruit- and plant-eating, and their day begins
just after dawn, when they set off through the forest to find
food. The gorillas eat as they walk along, but if they find a
ripe fruit tree, the younger ones will clamber into the
branches. When they need to digest, the gorillas build
day-nests on the ground and sleep for two or
three hours. The troop moves off again eating
and travelling until dusk. The silverback
decides when it is time to stop and each
gorilla builds a new nest for the night.

19th-century
engraving of a
gorilla family

HIGH CLIMBER
This young zoo gorilla
is playing on a climbing
frame. For many years,
scientists thought that
gorillas were too heavy
to climb trees, until they
actually studied them in
the wild. They found
that even adults are
surprisingly agile and
often climb high into
trees to reach ripe fruit.

*White tail tuft helps mother
locate infant in the jungle*

A QUICK BITE
Gorillas sometimes crouch on
two feet like this to gather up
fallen fruit, or when there is not
enough food in one place to make
it worth sitting down! It is also a
useful posture to adopt when
feeding on fierce soldier ants,
because it exposes less of the
body to their painful bites.

*Juvenile
has lost
its white
tail tuft*

*Nimble fingers
pick up fruit*

THE FEMALE ROLE
Mature females like this
one may be smaller than
the males, but their role
in the continuation of
the group is vital. Female
gorillas first give birth
when they are eight
years old, and the baby
gorillas are weaned
at the age of two.
Females may leave
their parents'
group and join
another group.
This avoids
in-breeding.

*Weight rests
on the knuckles
while walking*

A SLIMMER GORILLA

In the gorilla world, it is not unhealthy to have a pot belly. It just means that the owner eats a hearty diet of bulky vegetation. Many zoo gorillas (right) look much slimmer than those in the wild because they are often fed on pellets of concentrated food, and given fewer fruit and vegetables.

LIFE AT THE TOP

The big silverback is lord of all he surveys. Apart from making all the day-to-day decisions for the troop, he can also take his pick of the breeding females. Serious fights among male gorillas are infrequent, but the silverback may take exception to another male when he becomes fully mature at about 11 or 12 years. The younger male may decide to leave the troop, and he will live alone or with other males until he can form his own troop.

Bare chest is a sign of maturity

Young gorilla can watch the world go by from its safe perch

JUNGLE EXPLORER

A gorilla learns to walk at about five to six months. When it is 18 months old, like this young gorilla, it can follow its mother on foot for short distances, often resting one hand on her rump for security. By the time it is two, it has enough confidence to follow the troop on its own. However, the young gorilla stays close to its mother so it can climb on her back if it gets scared or tired.

Mother munches as she walks along

ON THE MOVE

The safest place for a young gorilla when travelling through the jungle is on its mother's back. From here it can watch the other members of the troop as they follow the broad silver back of the dominant male along the forest floor. Infant gorillas depend upon their mothers for transport until they are about two and a half or three years old, by which time they are strong enough to walk by themselves for fairly long distances.

Gorilla leans forwards to use his teeth on a stubborn plant

Pot belly is not an unhealthy sign

Food picked from the wayside

BREAKFAST IN BED

If food is within easy reach when a gorilla wakes up in its night-nest, it will have breakfast in bed before setting off into the forest. The silverback decides the pace and direction of the day's travel and will also indicate when it is time to stop and rest. Although he may look easy-going, the silverback is in fact keeping a constant look-out for dangers along the way.

Adapting to the dark

IN THE DARK OF AN AFRICAN NIGHT, the quiet background of insect noises may be pierced by a strange, child-like cry. This is the call of the bushbaby, or galago, a small, nocturnal primate. Bushbabies have sensitive, mobile ears to detect moving insects, and large eyes to focus on their prey in moonlight or starlight. They are very agile, moving quickly and leaping from branch to branch. At the opposite end of the speed scale, but related to the galago, are the loris, the potto, and the angwantibo. These strange, slow primates are also nocturnal and creep about the forest in search of fruit and creatures slow enough to be caught. There are no bushbabies in Asia, but there is a fast-moving nocturnal primate – the tarsier. With their huge eyes, the three species of tarsier all look like tiny gremlins. In one species, a single eye weighs more than the animal's brain!

PRIMATE OWL
In spite of their large appealing eyes and cute faces, tarsiers are efficient and ruthless predators. Hunting at night, they silently drop on to large insects, roosting birds, and even venomous snakes. They kill their prey with a nip of their sharp teeth, and meticulously finish off every edible morsel.

SLOW MOVER
A slender loris creeps through the trees, grasping branches with each hand and foot. Lorises eat the slow-moving caterpillars, beetles, and millipedes that faster insectivores leave behind.

Nocturnal spectral tarsier
Tarsius spectrum

Potto's specialized hand has small bump for second finger

A LEAP IN THE DARK
The nocturnal spectral tarsier is only the size of a squirrel, yet it can leap across gaps of 6 m (20 ft). Tarsiers spend most of their lives holding on to and jumping between upright stems, using the sticky pads on their toes to cling to even the smoothest wood. With their tails to prop themselves up, they can even sleep clinging to vertical branches.

Enlarged thumb

PINCER FINGERS
This plaster cast of the hand of a potto (*Parodicticus potto*) shows how the muscular thumb is set at 180 degrees opposite the other fingers. The hand works like a pincer, allowing the potto to grasp branches and small trees in a clamp-like grip.

Pincer-shaped hand can close tightly around branches

ALL EYES

The main feature of a loris' face are its eyes. Enormous eye sockets, or orbits, are set into the skull and protected by a thick, bony ring called the orbital margin.

Rounded cranium, or brain case

Post-orbital bar protects side of eye

CRUNCHY SUPPER

This lesser bushbaby is eating a praying mantis. After spending the day asleep, a bushbaby sets off to hunt as soon as it is dark. Its large, mobile ears are sensitive to the sounds made by insects, scorpions, spiders, lizards, or nesting birds. Bushbabies also eat fallen fruit, petals, nectar, and the sap of some trees.

Large, mobile ears for detecting movement of prey

Enormous eyes for keen night vision

SCENT SIGNALS

This greater bushbaby's powerfully built back legs suggest that it is a vertical clinger and leaper, like a tarsier. But scientists have found that different bushbaby species move in different ways. Some bushbabies move on all fours, while others seldom leap at all. However they move about their territory, bushbabies let others know of their presence by annointing their hands and feet with their own urine. In this way, every hand- and foothold leaves a smelly message that says clearly "I was here".

Long, powerful legs for gripping on to and leaping from branch to branch

Hand has six protective pads on palm

Relatively short arms, with hands for grabbing prey

IZING THE PATTERN

Zebras have the same pattern on their bodies. Zebras live in protective family groups and recognize family members by their patterns. The black-and-white stripes are also confusing to a predator when the zebra are moving, and help them escape animals, such as the lion, that are much faster.

CHAPTER 4
LIFE ON THE LAND

ALTHOUGH LIFE MAY SEEM to be uniformly
distributed over the surface of the earth, in reality
it is very uneven. In the extreme heat of some desert
areas, and in parts of the frozen continent of Antarctica,
there is no life at all. The complexity of life found in
other areas reflects the extraordinary variety of
habitats in which the animals and plants live.

CATCHING THE EYE
To survive, species must procreate,
and many animals, birds, and insects have
evolved spectacular courtship displays. The
male peacock, Pavo cristatus, spreads out
his long, colourful feathers in a shimmering
fan to impress a female. After the breeding
season is over, the long tail feathers fall out.

Clouds of all kinds

In 1803, THE ENGLISH pharmacist and amateur meteorologist Luke Howard identified ten categories of cloud. All these are variations on three basic cloud forms – puffy cumulus clouds, layered stratus clouds, and feathery cirrus clouds. This system proved so simple and effective that it is still used by meteorologists today. Clouds form whenever moist air is lifted high enough above the ground to cool and condense. Cumulus clouds form because the sun heats the ground unevenly. In some places this creates bubbles of warm air, thermals, that drift upwards through the cooler air. As they rise, the bubbles cool until, high up, water vapour condenses to form a cloud.

FLYING SAUCERS
Lenticular clouds, so-called because they look like lenses, always form in the lee of mountains.

TRANSLUCENT CLOUD
Altostratus are high, thin sheets of cloud that can often completely cover the sky, so that the sun looks as if it is seen through misty glass. Altostratus usually appear at a warm front, where warm, moist air from the tropics slides up over a wedge of cold, polar air. The lower, thicker, nimbostratus rain clouds follow.

Strong updraughts carry billows of cloud high into the atmosphere

Temperature here –40°C (–40°F)

FLEECY CLOUDS
Altocumulus are puffs and rolls of cloud, visible at medium heights. Unlike the higher, smaller cirrocumulus, they often have dark, shadowed sides.

A GREY BLANKET
Stratus is a vast, dull type of cloud that hangs low over the ground and may produce a damp drizzle, but no real rain. Higher up, on hills or even from tall buildings, stratus simply appears as fog.

Temperature here 0°C (32°F)

Cirrus — 12
Cirrostratus — 11
Cirrocumulus — 10
— 9
Altostratus — 8
Altocumulus — 7
Stratocumulus — 6
— 5
Cumulus — 4
Cumulonimbus — 3
Stratus — 2
Nimbostratus — 1

Sea level (km)

CLOUD HEIGHTS
Cirrus-type clouds, including cirrocumulus and cirrostratus, form at the top of the troposphere, where it is coldest. Altostratus and altocumulus are found at medium heights; stratocumulus, stratus, nimbostratus, and cumulus form closer to the ground. Cumulonimbus may reach up through the whole troposphere.

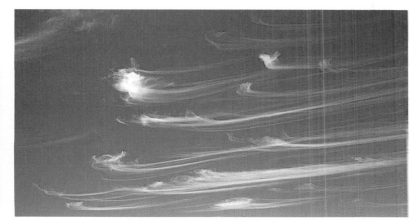

TRAILING VIRGA
Cumulus clouds sometimes let rain or ice crystals fall into drier, slower-moving layers of air. The streaks that result known as virga, evaporate before they reach the ground, and from below look as if they are vanishing into thin air.

MARES' TAILS
Cirrus clouds form high in the sky where the atmosphere is so cold that they are made entirely from ice crystals. Strong winds blow the crystals into wispy "mares' tails".

AN ICY VEIL
Cirrostratus occur when cirrus clouds spread into a thin, milky sheet. The sun appears very bright and may have one or more coloured rings, or haloes, around it and, occasionally, brilliant "mock suns".

HIGH, FLUFFY CLOUDS
Cirrocumulus are tiny, high clumps of shadowless clouds. They consist of ice crystals, like all cirrus clouds, and often form in beautiful, regular waves and ripples known as a mackerel sky – because they look like the mottled scales of the mackerel.

Typical anvil shape

Mixture of ice crystals and water

A LAYER OF CUMULUS
Stratocumulus often form when the tops of cumulus clouds rise and spread out sideways into broad sheets. Viewed from an aeroplane, they appear as an undulating blanket of cloud, with narrow breaks that sometimes allow a glimpse of the ground.

CLOUDS THAT BRING SHOWERS
Bigger and darker than cumulus, cumulonimbus usually bring rain showers – nimbus means "rain" in Latin. Sometimes they grow huge and unleash sudden, dramatic thunderstorms.

Violent updraughts and downdraughts in front wall of cloud create hailstones

CAULIFLOWER CLOUDS
Cumulus clouds often mass together and grow upward. They have dense, white heads that look just like cauliflowers. If they keep on growing, they may become rain-bearing cumulonimbus.

Mainly water droplets

Air drawn in here

Natural signs

WHAT'S THE WEATHER LIKE?
Everyone from travellers to sailors had to know about the weather and be aware of natural signs around them.

NOTHING BUT A GROUNDHOG
In the United States, 2 February is Groundhog Day. People say that if a groundhog sees its shadow, the weather will remain cold for six more weeks. Weather records have proved the groundhog wrong many times.

SAILORS, FARMERS, AND OTHERS whose livelihood depends on the weather learned long ago that the world around them gives all kinds of clues to the weather to come – as long as they know what to look for. Age-old advice passed down from generation to generation has been offered on everything from the colour of the sky to the feel of your boots in the morning. Of course, most country weather lore is little more than superstition and all but useless for weather forecasting. But some is based on close observation of the natural world and can give an accurate prediction of the weather. Tiny variations in the air, which humans cannot feel, often affect plants and animals. A change in their behaviour or appearance can be a sign of a change in the weather.

SUNDAY OPENING
The scarlet pimpernel is often known as the "poor man's weather glass". Its tiny flowers open wide in sunny weather, but close up when rain is in the air.

Sunset

Sunrise

SEEING RED
Old country wisdom says: *Red sky at night, shepherds' delight; red sky in the morning, shepherds' warning.* This means a fiery sunset should be followed by a fine morning, and a fiery dawn by storms. Weather experts are doubtful.

Kelp is sensitive to changes in humidity

WOOLLY WARNING
Wool is very responsive to the humidity of the air. When the air is dry, wool shrinks and curls up. If rain is on its way, the air is moist, and wool swells and straightens out.

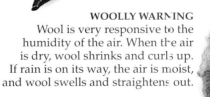

WEATHER WEED
People near the sea often hang out strands of kelp, because seaweed is one of the best natural weather forecasters. In fine weather, the kelp shrivels and is dry to the touch. If rain threatens, the weed swells and feels damp.

Cone in wet weather   Cone in dry weather

INSECT FORECASTING
Like many small creatures, grasshoppers are sensitive to changes in the weather, chirruping louder and louder as the temperature rises. The chirruping is not actually a song, but the sound of the grasshoppers' hind legs rubbing rapidly against their hard front wings.

WEATHER CONES
A pine cone is a very reliable natural weather indicator. In dry weather, the scales on the pine cone open out; when they close up, it is a good sign that rain is on the way. This is because, in dry weather, the scales shrivel and stand out stiffly. When the air is damp, the scales absorb moisture and become pliable again, allowing the cone to regain its normal shape.

Oak   Ash

GLORIOUS MORNING
Like the scarlet pimpernel, the petals of the flower morning glory open and shut in response to weather conditions. These wide-open blooms indicate fine weather.

SOAK OR SPLASH?
According to some country weather lore, natural signs can indicate the weather, not just for the next few hours but for many days to come. There is an old saying, for instance, that says: *If the oak flowers before the ash, we shall have a splash* (meaning only light rain for the next month or so). *If the ash flowers before the oak, we shall have a soak* (meaning very wet weather). There is little evidence, however, to support these long-range predictions.

LYING COWS
When cows lie down in a field, it is often said that rain must be on the way. Apparently, the cows sense the dampness in the air and are making sure they have somewhere dry to lie. While many animals can indeed sense changes in the weather before humans, this particular prediction is proved wrong as often as right.

SPRING IS HERE
Many natural signs are said to herald the end of winter, such as the first blooming of the white flowers of the horse chestnut. It is true that the flowers only appear when the weather is mild – but this is no guarantee that there will be no more winter storms.

WINTER'S TAIL
Some country folk expect a severe winter if in autumn squirrels have very bushy tails, or gather big stores of nuts. But scientists have found no evidence to support this.

Fiery rocks

WHEN VOLCANOES ERUPT, they may bleed rivers of red-hot lava or spew great clouds of ash and gas into the atmosphere. Sometimes the lava oozes gently from a hole in the ground. At other times, it is thrown into the air in spectacular fire fountains that run together when they land. In either case, the lava flows off the volcano in rivers of hot rock that may spread out and cover the countryside before it cools. Fire fountains and lava flows are common in Iceland and Hawaii. They are quite easy to predict in these areas, and it is often possible to get near them and photograph them in close-up. However, from time to time, volcanic gas escapes from the hot rock and this may cause explosions that throw out bombs and blocks – chunks of flying lava that litter the ground around the vent.

Weedy, flowering plant

Two species of moss

Lichen

GATHERING MOSS
How quickly lava is re-colonized by plants depends on the nature of the erupted material. The climate and altitude are also important – recolonization is fastest in the tropics, for example. This piece of lava is from a flow on the west slope of Mount Vesuvius in Italy after an eruption in 1944. Some 50 years later, lichen covers much of the flow, and moss, grasses, and weedy flowering plants are taking root.

BOMBS AND BLOCKS
Bombs and blocks can be as big as houses or as small as tennis balls. Bombs are usually more rounded, while blocks are more dense and angular. Their shapes depend upon how molten or gassy the lava was during flight. Very liquid chunks of lava plop to the ground like cow pats; denser, more solid ones often shatter as they land.

Bomb thrown out by Mount Etna, and covered with red crust of hematite

SPITTING MOUNTAIN
One of the highest mountains and most active volcanoes in Europe, Mount Etna rises 3,390 m (11,122 ft) over the Italian island of Sicily. Its barren summit is almost always bubbling with lava. Lava flows from an unusually long eruption destroyed several houses and threatened villages in 1992.

Small, explosive eruption photographed at night on Mount Etna

Dense, round bomb

Odd twists and tails of many bombs formed as they spin through the air

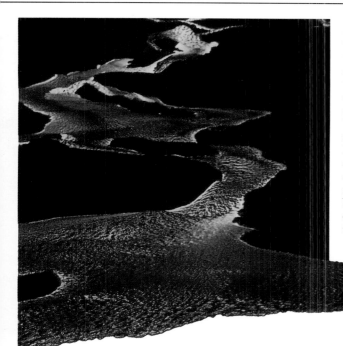

AA FLOWS
Glowing red at night, the intense heat of an aa flow shows through the surface crust of cooling lava. The flow moves forward like a bulldozer track, as solidifying blocks of lava drop down the advancing front and are run over Lava flows cool very slowly because rock is a poor conductor of heat. As they harden, the lava flows slow down and grow thicker.

PAHOEHOE FLOWS
Pahoehoe is more fluid than aa and contains more gas. As its surface cools, the flow grows a thin, pliable skin. The hot lava on the inside distorts the skin, wrinkling it so that its surface looks like the coil of a rope. The skin of a pahoehoe flow may crust over into a roof thick enough to walk on. Only a metre or so below, hot lava continues to run in a tunnel or tube.

Hardened chunk of pahoehoe lava

Lava flows

Lava flows pose little danger to people as they rarely travel faster than a few kilometres an hour. The two kinds of flows get their names from Hawaiian words. Aa (pronounced *ah-ah*) flows are covered in sharp, angular chunks of lava known as scoria. Pahoehoe (*pa-hoy-hoy*) flows grow a smooth skin soon after they leave the vent. Pahoehoe flows are rarely more than 1 m (3.3 ft) thick, while the thickest aa flows may be 100 m (330 ft) high.

Driblets of remelted lava from roof of a pahoehoe tunnel

Chunk of scoria from surface of an aa flow

PAHOEHOE TOE
This picture shows red-hot pahoehoe bulging through a crack in its own skin. New skin is forming over the bulge. A pahoehoe flow creeps forward with thousands of little breakouts like this one. The chilled surface of the flow traps gas, keeping the flows in the tunnels hot and mobile. The lava often travels many kilometres from the vent in this way, engulfing fertile land and villages as it goes.

FIRE AND WATER
Volcanic islands like Hawaii and Iceland are usually fringed by black beaches. The sand is formed when hot lava hits the sea and is shattered into tiny, glassy particles. It is black because the lava is rich in dark minerals like iron oxides, and low in light-coloured ones like quartz.

Black sand from volcanic island of Santorini, Greece

On the mountainside

THE HIGHER THE ALTITUDE at which a plant grows or an animal lives, the colder are the temperatures it has to endure. The thin air holds little heat, and on exposed mountainsides, high winds create a chill factor which makes the cold even more penetrating. In addition, low rainfall and thin, frozen soils mean that water is scarce. However, mountain (alpine) plants are generally small and compact so they can survive on high mountain peaks, often growing in dense cushions or flattened mats to give them protection against the cold, drying wind. Animals and insects live on all levels of a mountain, sometimes moving between different levels in search of food or greater warmth.

Canada lynx

Large neck ruff

Western Himalayan spruce
Picea smithiana

HIMALAYAN CONIFER
Above the tropical forests of the southern Himalayan slopes are mixed forests that contain many coniferous trees. This elegant spruce is found on the middle slopes. It has a narrow crown and drooping shoots, and the cones have smooth, notched scales.

MOUNTAIN RANGES
There are mountains on all the continents. A few form great mountain ranges, such as the Rocky Mountains and the Himalayas. On the highest peaks of mountain ranges, snow lies frozen all year round. Below the high mountaintops with their snowy peaks, alpine meadows, and scrub are the cool coniferous forests and waterlogged moorlands. On the lower slopes, the warmer, deciduous forests are home to many animals and insects.

Lady
Amherst's
pheasant
*Chrysolophus
Amherstiae*

SEASONAL MIGRATION
Hardy pheasants such as this spectacular Lady Amherst's pheasant live in the mountain forests of Asia. They move up and down the mountains with the seasons. This shy, secretive bird rarely emerges from the bamboo thickets and dense forest where it lives. It eats bamboo shoots as well as small animals, insects, and spiders. It sometimes fishes under stones in streams for small aquatic animals.

*Male has long
and colourful tail
feathers for display*

Himalayan
Mazus reptans
grows in mats

Bhutan Glory
Bhutanitis lidderdalei

Alpine daphne, or
garland flower, is
a miniature shrub

MOUNTAIN BEAUTY
Many butterflies and moths
have adapted to the harsh
climate of mountains. This
Bhutan Glory lives in the high
mountain forests of Thailand and
India. It is a dark brown because darker
colours absorb sunlight more easily, so the
insect can warm up rapidly in the early
morning, when the air temperature is low.

Butterfly has prominent
eyespots to startle
predatory birds

Mosihias have
small leaves to
withstand high winds

Female mountain gorilla
Gorilla gorilla
beringei

Brilliant colours of
North American phlox
stand out to attract
pollinating insects

This St John's wort
is much smaller
than its lowland
relatives

Weight rests
on knuckles
when walking

ALPINE PLANTS
Many plants have adapted to the harsh climate
of high mountains. Some alpine plants, such as
Mazus reptans, are "prostrate", or mat-forming.
Others are simply smaller than similar species
in warmer habitats. The leaves are often small
and tough to resist sharp frosts, and some are
covered with fine hairs to protect them from the
sun's ultraviolet rays, which are more intense at
these heights. Mountain summers are short, so
the plants have to flower and produce seeds
quickly before the cold weather returns.

MOUNTAIN APE
Mountain gorillas live in the mountain forest of the Virunga volcanoes in
Africa. Their thick fur keeps out the chill, while water runs off the outer
layer of hairs. Mothers like this pregnant female wrap their shaggy arms
round their babies to keep them warm and dry. Gorillas spend most of their
time on the ground, but will often climb trees to search for fruit, bark, or
leaves. Today, there are fewer than 650 mountain gorillas left in the world.

Lords of the skies

THE HUGE SUMMER BREEDING COLONIES of birds in both the Arctic and the Antarctic attract a number of predatory birds quick to enjoy the easy meals of eggs and chicks. In the Arctic, the small mammals of the tundra lands, such as lemmings and hares, increase the range of food for birds to hunt. The variety of predatory birds is therefore greater in the Arctic than in the Antarctic and includes eagles, skuas, owls, falcons, and buzzards. The predators' own breeding cycle coincides with that of their prey – a way of ensuring that their chicks will have plenty to eat.

GHOSTLY HUNTER
Snowy owls feed largely on the millions of lemmings living on the Arctic tundra, and their population is closely linked to the regular three- to four-year rise and fall in lemming numbers. Many of these superb owls wander far south in winter.

Soapstone and ivory owl carved by Inuit craftsman in Cape Dorset, Canada

Feathers at tips of wings spread out like fingers to help the eagle push and steer through the air

Spread feathers help the bird to reduce speed

Powerful wings give both speed and control in flight

Lethal curved talons grip, crush, and carry off prey

Strong legs to cushion impact of landing

The golden eagle slows in midair and spreads out its wings and tail to act as a brake

Eyes firmly focused on its destination, the eagle further brakes its flight by swinging out its lower body and legs

At the last moment, its feet swing down to grip the perch

WATCH OUT BELOW
Golden eagles fly at low altitudes while hunting, then swoop suddenly to pounce on their prey. This swoop-and-grab attack is effective because it happens so swiftly that the prey is often taken unawares. Here, a golden eagle is landing on a branch in much the same way as it would when diving for the next meal.

KING OF THE CLOUDS

As the most powerful and majestic bird in the sky, the eagle features in countless stories, myths, and legends. Here a magnificent eagle perches in a tree in an illustration by British illustrator Reginald Knowles. It forms the title page of a collection of Norse legends.

Keen eyesight to spot birds and animals moving on the ground below

Powerful hooked bill to tear flesh from prey

Golden eagle
Aquila chrysaetos

Huge chest muscles drive the enormous wings

Gyrfalcon
Falco rusticolus

A KILLING MACHINE

A magnificent flier, the golden eagle is a fierce predator of ptarmigan and other birds as well as small mammals such as ground squirrels and hares. Golden eagles usually kill their prey before carrying it off in their strong talons. They sometimes hunt in pairs, especially in winter.

BIGGEST AND BEST

The most powerful of the falcons, the gyrfalcon relies on power and speed to catch its victims. They usually kill their prey in flight.

FALCON FOOD

The rock ptarmigan (*Lagopus mutus*) is the gyrfalcon's main prey.

Mountain weather

Hɪɢʜ ᴜᴘ ɪɴ ᴛʜᴇ ᴀᴛᴍᴏsᴘʜᴇʀᴇ, pressure drops, winds are ferocious, and the air is bitterly cold. On mountain tops, such as that of Mount Everest, the air pressure is very low, winds howl through the crags at up to 320 km/h (192 mph), and the temperature often drops to –70°C (–94°F). Because mountains jut so far into the atmosphere, they interfere with wind and cloud patterns, forcing air to move up or down as it passes over the peaks. Air rising up the windward side of a mountain means that the lower summits are often shrouded in mist and rain.

CLOUDS AND SNOW
In many mountain ranges, the highest peaks project above the tops of the clouds, basking in bright sunshine while clouds fill the valley below. However, though sunny, the peaks are usually icy cold and any heat from the sun is reflected straight back into the atmosphere by the snow. Near the equator, only the very highest peaks – above 5,000 m (16,400 ft) – are perpetually covered in snow, as it is too cold for rain. Towards the poles, however, the snow line gets progressively lower.

HIGH READINGS
Many weather stations are sited on the tops of mountains to record conditions high up in the atmosphere. On the summit of Mount Washington in New Hampshire in the United States, winds are frequently over 160 km/h (96 mph), and temperatures are often below –30°C (–22°F).

MEASURING AIR PRESSURE
In 1648, a French scientist, Blaise Pascal, proved that the atmosphere had its own weight, or pressure. Pascal reasoned that the air pressure would be lower at the top of a mountain, because there was less air weighing down on it from above. When he took a barometer up a mountain the mercury level showing air pressure dropped as expected.

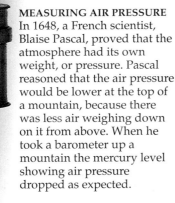

Barometer used for measuring air pressure

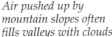
Air pushed up by mountain slopes often fills valleys with clouds

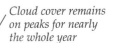
Cloud cover remains on peaks for nearly the whole year

WET AT THE TOP
Even when they are not particularly cold, the tops of mountain are often wet and misty – especially if they poke up into a moist air stream. Pacific island mountains, like these in Tahiti, are among the dampest places in the world. Hawaii's Mount Wai-'ale-'ale is wreathed in moist clouds for 354 days a year. It is also soaked annually by more than 11,600 mm (457 in) of rain.

Barometer
very low

A little
cloud
cover

Winds of
155 km/h
(99 mph)
or more

ADAPTING

Tiny flowers
called alpines
have been
very successful
in adapting to
the sunny, cold
weather of
mountain ranges
such as the Alps
in Europe,
where they grow
plentifully in spring.

HIGH SIERRA

High up in the mountains, there is often a
strong wind which increases the chilling effect,
even on sunny days. Mountain tops are usually
much more windy than open, low country. This
is partly because wind strength can be much
stronger at 1,000 m (3,280 ft) than at sea level.
Winds also rush over, rather than around, the
tops of mountains, and gain speed as they go.

*Air warms and dries
as it descends*

Leeward
side

Rain on summit

Windward
side

*Moist air
forced upwards
by mountain range*

*Rising air cools and
condenses into clouds*

RISING AIR

When a moist air stream meets a
mountain range, it is forced upwards towards the
summit. As it rises, it cools and may condense into clouds
around the top. Higher-level clouds can then act as "feeder"
clouds, letting a little rain fall onto the summit clouds below.
Warm fronts may be broken up when they run up against a
mountain ridge, while cold fronts may deposit so much rain that
they die out quickly on the far side. All this brings rain to the
windward side of mountains, and leaves the leeward side drier.

In the rainforest

TROPICAL RAINFORESTS contain more species and a greater diversity of colourful plant and animal life than any other habitat on earth. These forests are found in permanently wet, warm areas near the equator, where there is at least 1,500 mm (60 in) of rain a year. The jungles have three layers – an evergreen canopy in the middle, a layer of smaller plants on the forest floor and, towering above the canopy, scattered taller trees known as emergents. At all levels of the rainforest there is a host of wary creatures with a strong instinct for survival. In the canopy, many metres above the ground, harpy eagles swoop on their prey. Lower down, hungry pitcher plants digest the insects that fall into their cups. In the dim light of the forest floor, scorpions and other poisonous creatures scuttle and slither their way through the maze of roots, fallen leaves, and dying branches.

A NASTY SHOCK
There are many ways in which rainforest creatures protect themselves. Any predator that tries to sample this spiky leaf insect will receive a painful surprise because the insect has sharp spines all over its body. This female is an immature nymph, its wings not yet fully formed.

Tomato frogs
Dyscophis antongili

RAINFORESTS IN DANGER
Madagascar, off the southeast coast of Africa, is the world's fourth largest island. Like many other islands (pp. 122–123), most of its rainforest wildlife has evolved in isolation and is unique. However, many of the plants and animals, such as the rare comet orchid (*Angraecum sesquipedale)* and these tomato frogs, are endangered as a result of the forests being cut down and burned by farmers to clear the way for agriculture.

Four simple eyes on each side of the head

LIVING DANGEROUSLY
Heavy with moisture, the air near the shady forest floor is still and sultry. The poisonous tiger centipede is typical of the creatures that are well hidden in the dense vegetation. Tiger centipedes emerge only at night, when the forest is cool and damp. They have large poison claws just below the head, and feed on insects and spiders, as well as small toads and mammals.

Postman butterfly
Heliconius melpomene

When not in use, proboscis is curled up under head

WARNING
The black and red colours of the postman butterfly warn birds that this is not a tasty meal. The butterfly feeds on nectar and pollen, sucking them up through its long proboscis. The females lay their eggs on the young leaves of the poisonous passion flower (*Passiflora*). The larvae absorb the poison from the plant into their bodies.

Fig leaf
Ficus religiosa

SELF-DEFENCE
Tropical Asia includes many countries and encompasses an enormous area, all of it rich in animal and plant life. The term "jungle" comes from a Hindi word meaning "impenetrable forest and undergrowth around settlements", and there is nothing more impenetrable than the climbing palms called rattans. There are 600 species of rattans, 69 of which are found in the Philippines alone. The tall palms reach the canopy by means of barbed whips on the tips of fronds clothed with hooked spikes. Despite these vicious devices, the flexible rattan stems are cultivated to make cane furniture, fish traps, and hammocks, while the young shoots are eaten, and the juice from the fruits is used as a dye or medicine to treat rheumatism and other ailments.

Drip tip

DRIP TIPS
Many rainforest leaves have a shiny, waxy surface, and are drawn out into a narrow point, or drip tip. Both these features are designed to encourage rainwater to run off the leaves quickly, so preventing the growth of minute algae, liverworts, and fungi, which might weigh down the leaves.

Rattan palm
Calamus caesius

Tiger centipede
Scolopendra gigantea

Living on the grasslands

MUCH OF THE AFRICAN continent is grassland, and most areas are hot savannah plains lying between tropical forests and desert land. Grasses, small trees, and shrubs are scattered across the savannah, with tall, thick grasses growing near the forests, and shorter, thinner grasses near the deserts. Grazing animals such as zebra, antelope, and wildebeest live in large herds that wander the plains cropping the grass as they go. The trees and shrubs, such as the acacias, have deep roots to reach water sources underground, and provide nourishment for many of the herbivores that live on the grasslands. Large browsing animals use their different heights to reach different parts of the foliage. The giraffes eat the tasty shoots at the top, the elephants the leaves, twigs, and bark, and the black rhinoceros the lower branches. The water in the acacia leaves keeps these animals hydrated in this dry area – the animals sometimes go up to a week without drinking.

Males' skulls strengthened for fighting

Small horns

Patas monkey
Erythrocebus patas

Cloven hoof like that of a cow

Males are twice as big as females

Long legs for sprinting

LIVING IN A HERD
Giraffes live herds of up to 12 individuals that may be very spread out over a wide area, but move together across the plains. The males average 5 m (16 ft) in height and weigh 1,400 kg (3,080 lb), while the females are about 4.3 m (14 ft) tall and around 800 kg (1,760 lb). Giraffes move with some difficulty. They have trouble getting up from the ground when resting, but when they gallop away, few predators can catch them. Unlike most large animals, they move with both legs on the same side moving together, and they gallop for hours without getting tired.

PLAINS MONKEY
The patas monkey, also known as the military monkey because of its reddish coat and impressive white moustache, lives on the dry plains of Africa in troops of around 15 to 20 monkeys. It lives on the ground and its long legs mean that it can bound along at 55 km/h (33 mph) if necessary. Patas troops spend most of the day moving around looking for leaves, fruit, and flowers to eat. At night, the monkeys climb into trees to sleep.

Spongy blood vessels near brain prevent blood pressure problems when giraffe bends down to drink

Reticulated giraffe
Giraffa melopardis

Zebra
Equus burchelli

Because of its long neck, giraffe has to lower or raise head slowly

RECORD HEIGHTS

No animal alive today is as tall as a giraffe. The long neck evolved to enable the animal to browse on the foliage of trees on the wide plains of the savannah. The extraordinary thing about a giraffe's neck is that it contains only seven vertebrae – exactly the same number as there are in the necks of the other mammals, including our own. The vertebrae are simply long – 0.3 m (1 ft) long. When it reaches into the tree tops, the giraffe's long tongue grasps leaves and twigs and pulls them within reach. The canine teeth have two deep grooves to strip the leaves from their twigs.

HERDING TOGETHER

The main threat to the large herds of zebra on the African plains, apart from drought, is the efficient hunting of the large cats – the lion, leopard, and cheetah. Lions hunt in groups. The lionesses do most of the work picking out and attacking the weakest animals in the herd, so zebras stay together as this gives them better protection. Zebra herds contain family groups of around 12 females and their foals led by a dominant male. By day, they graze on the long, coarse grass and drink from water-holes regularly. They migrate to find water in the dry season.

Ostrich
Struthio camelus

Flexible neck

BIG BIRD

The ostrich is the heaviest bird, 90–156 kg (200–345 lb), the tallest bird, 2.1–2.7 m (7–9 ft), and the fastest two-legged animal, up to 75 km/h (45 mph), in the world. It also lays the largest egg, which has an incredible average weight of 1.5 kg (3.3 lb). The ostrich lays between 6 and 20 eggs at one time, and incubates them for up to 48 days. Ostriches are omnivorous, eating grass, seeds, insects, and small animals.

How plants survive in the desert

Plants that live in deserts either spring up from dormant seeds after rain, or stay alive all year by adapting to the meagre supply of water. The more permanent plants have a variety of ways in which they obtain water. Some have long roots to reach moisture deep in the soil, some spread their roots to collect water over a wide area, while others absorb dew through their leaves. Many desert plants, including cacti, are succulents that are able to store water. A thick waxy layer on the stems and leaves helps retain moisture and protects tissues from the sun's intense heat. Growing smaller leaves, shedding leaves in times of drought, or even having no leaves at all, also helps reduce water loss by keeping the surface area of the plant to a minimum.

DATE PALMS
This grove of date palms is at an oasis in Oman. Only female trees produce dates, so just a few male trees are grown to produce pollen. Palm trees can live for up to 200 years.

Very long roots to seek out water

FLESHY LEAF
Haworthias grow in places with some shade, usually next to rocks. Only the tip of the leaves poke above the surface of the soil, to keep the rest out of the sun. But leaves need light to be able to make food by photosynthesis. This leaf has a translucent (clear) window in the tip to allow light through the leaf.

These agaves with varied patterns have been specially bred

FRESH DATES
There are many different varieties of dates. The most familiar are the ones that are dried and packed in boxes for export around the world. Dried dates are also part of the staple diet of villagers and desert nomads such as the Bedouin. They are highly nutritious and do not rot easily.

CENTURY PLANTS
It takes 20 to 50 years for the century plant to produce flowers on a stem up to 30 ft (9 m) tall which grows out of the centre of the plant. The flowers are pollinated by nectar-seeking bats. After flowering and producing seeds the plant dies. The century plant belongs to the agave family, members of which are a source of sweet sap for drinks, and fibres for ropes and other products.

FIRE THORN BRANCH
Also called the ocotillo, or coachwhip plant, the fire thorn grows in the deserts of the south-western USA. In dry times, it sheds its leaves to conserve moisture. After rains, new leaves grow among the spines; if the ground is wet enough the fire thorn flowers.

WELWITSCHIA
This bizarre plant has only two frayed, strap-like leaves, and a huge tap root which may be up to 3.3 ft (1 m) wide at the top. It grows on the gravel plains in the Namib Desert. Welwitschia is actually a dwarf tree, and may live for one hundred years or more, each leaf growing about 5 cm (2 in) a year.

Leaf absorbs dew

Welwitschia leaves usually split into many strips

When spread out, each leaf reaches up to 2 m (6.5 ft) long

Thick, waxy layer
also protects tissue
of cactus from
burning effects
of the strong sun

Sharp spines

*Water-storing
tissue*

BARREL CACTUS

A cactus is well adapted to make the most of
any water available. Inside, there is a mass of water-
storing tissue. The surface of the cactus is covered with
a thick waxy layer which helps prevent loss of moisture,
and the shallow roots spread out around the plant to
absorb rain or dew. Desert cacti open their stomata
(pores) at night to exchange gases for respiration and
photosynthesis (the manufacture of food from carbon
dioxide and water using sunlight). Carbon dioxide is
stored in another chemical form until it is ready to be
used during daylight for photosynthesis (pp. 40–41).

LIFE-GIVING DEW

Dew from coastal fog has settled
on a salt bush in the Namib Desert.
For plants and animals, dew is a
vital source of water. Some shrubs
are coated with salt; this is thought
to help the plant take in more
moisture from the fog.

LIVING STONES

Stone plants are often
hard to spot as they are so well
camouflaged. This saves them from plant-
eating animals. Stone plants are succulents – that is, they
store water in their leaves. They grow with all but the tips
of their leaves in the ground, and the surrounding soil and
stones protect them from intense sunlight. To allow light
to reach the underground part of the leaf, the surface of
the leaf tips have translucent windows. After the rains,
stone plants bloom, and produce a single large flower
between the leaf pair. They grow in southern Africa.

*Shallow,
spreading roots*

LIVING WITHOUT LEAVES

This spike of flowers in the
Jordanian desert belongs to
the leafless cistanche plant. It
does not need green leaves for
photosynthesis because it taps
the roots of other plants for
food. Living organisms
like the cistanche plant, that
steal food and harm their
hosts, are called parasites.

*Frayed, dried
end to leaf*

Desert wildlife

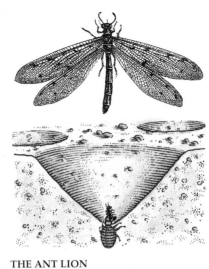

ANIMALS IN THE DESERT have a particular problem to solve because they have to find water in such a dry, dusty environment. Some plant-eating animals and insects feed on fresh green plants that spring up after rain. Others get moisture and food from prey or from dew. To avoid the drying effects of the sun, many desert creatures are only active at night. Desert hedgehogs and foxes spend the heat of the day in burrows, emerging when it is dark to search for food. Members of the cat family that live in desert regions often hunt at night, sheltering in rocky lairs or any available shade during the day. Some animals, however, such as the meerkat, are active during the day and dive into burrows when threatened by a predator. There are desert animals that avoid the driest times, only becoming active after occasional rains. The eggs of desert crustaceans, such as brine and tadpole shrimps, need water to bring them to life. In the dry season, spadefoot toads remain inactive, buried in the soil, only emerging when they hear rain drumming.

THE ANT LION
The larva of this winged insect is called an ant lion. As soon as it hatches, it digs a pit in the sand and hides at the bottom with only its jaws exposed, waiting for an insect such as an ant to come into the pit. When prey gets close enough, the ant lion flicks sand at it to make it lose its footing and slide down to certain death.

Long antenna

Jewel wasp

JEWEL OF THE DESERT
The hunting jewel wasps are solitary wasps, living on their own rather than in colonies. The adults feed on nectar from flowers, but their young eat cockroaches caught for them by the adult female. She hunts down the cockroach, stings it to paralyse it, and then drags the insect into a hole where she lays an egg on it. When the young hatches, it feeds on the paralyzed but alive cockroach.

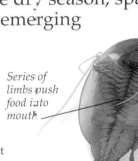

Series of limbs push food into mouth

Shield

Tadpole shrimps are 3 cm (1.2 in) in length

THIRSTY SHRIMPS
The eggs of these tadpole shrimps survive in dry sands for ten years or more before rain comes to bring them to life. The shrimps must grow quickly to reach maturity and produce eggs before the desert pool in which they live dries up and they die. Not all the eggs hatch the first time round. Some eggs are left for the next rains, in case the pools dry out, and the first shrimps die before they can complete their life cycle.

Distinctive ear tuft similar to that of lynx

DESERT CAT
The caracal lives in a wide range of habitats, including the deserts of Africa and Asia. These soft-footed cats are adept at catching birds, and can even leap into the air to swat a bird in flight. They also hunt reptiles, small mammals, and even larger prey such as gazelles. Caracals sleep in caves, rocky crevices, and the abandoned burrows of other animals.

Caracal
Lynx caracal

Desert hedgehog
*Paraechinus
aethiopicus*

Meerkat
Suricata suricatta

*A group of
meerkats is
capable of seeing
off a jackal or cobra*

LIVING TOGETHER

Meerkats live in the Kalahari and
Namib deserts, and in dry open
country in other parts of southern
Africa. They work together as a
group. A meerkat with its head
down looking for food in the
wide-open desert is an easy target
for a bird of prey, so one member
of each group scans the horizon
from a high place – on a raised
sandbank, or up a bush or tree. If a
predator is spotted, the guard barks in
alarm and the group races to the safety
of a burrow. There are nanny meerkats
in each group that take it in turns to look
after the young while the mothers are out
feeding with the rest of the group.

DESERT HEDGEHOG

This spiny creature lives in the dry regions of
northern Africa, the Arabian peninsula, and Iraq.
When threatened, like other species of hedgehog,
it rolls up to expose the spines of its coat, in order
to protect its vulnerable underparts. Desert
hedgehogs dig individual burrows which they
live in during the day. In the breeding season,
the female looks after the young in the burrow,
suckling them for two months. Adult hedgehogs
eat birds, eggs, scorpions, and small mammals.

*Enlarged glands
secrete a strong
poison to deter
predators*

Green toad
Bufo viridis

TOADS IN THE HEAT

Green toads live in oases where there is
a permanent water supply in which to
lay their eggs. During the day, they hide
under stones away from the heat of the
desert. At night, they emerge to hunt
insects near water holes and around
palm trees. They have enlarged glands
that secrete a strong poison that
tastes nasty and deters predators.

Island life

Many islands in the Pacific and Indian Oceans are created by the flow of volcanic lava or emerge from the sea at the summit of coral reefs. Once formed, these isolated chunks of land are populated by turtles, birds, and other sea wanderers. Some small invertebrates and seeds, for example those of the coconut, float there by sea, while other creatures and plants establish themselves after being carried by birds, blown by the wind, or transported by swimming reptiles. Because of their isolation, island populations often evolve into unique forms. Many birds become flightless, like the Galápagos cormorant and the almost flightless kakapo of New Zealand. Because there is plenty to eat and there are few predators, many island-dwellers grow to a great size. But their isolation also makes them vulnerable to invaders, such as the cats and rats introduced by people.

Coconut husk broken by robber crab **Birgo latus**

Powerful claws to crack open coconuts

Strengthened carapace

Cook islander holding a robber crab

ROBBER OF THE TREES
The robber or "coconut" crab is found on some Pacific islands. This giant crustacean has adapted to its environment by developing the ability to climb trees in search of coconuts, which it cracks open with powerful claws. As a young adult, the crab carries a mollusc shell, like a hermit crab, and when it has outgrown this, it carries half a coconut! Eventually, it relies on its claws and hardened exoskeleton for protection. On some islands, the crab is hunted for food. When caught, however, the robber crab must be held carefully, as the Cook islander is demonstrating (left), because it can inflict serious injury.

Leaf insect is
7 cm (2.75 in)
long

Leg

LEAF WITH LEGS
This leaf insect lives on the
island of Java, and is very well
camouflaged. Its skin has both the
colour and texture of a real leaf. There are
marks which resemble the midrib and veins
of a typical leaf, and it even has brown markings
that make it look like a leaf that is dying.

Eyelid can be closed
to tiny peephole

Chameleon
protected by
ability to change
colour to match
background

Toes
grouped
with two
on outside
and three on
inside of hand

Toes grouped
with three on
outside and two
on inside of foot

Cassowaries make a
threatening, booming
noise to scare invaders

FLIGHTLESS
Cassowaries, like
many island birds,
have lost the ability to fly.
They have powerful legs for
running and fighting, and dagger-like claws
for defence, and so do not need to fly away.
These solitary birds melt easily into the dense
jungles of New Guinea in the Pacific, where
they feed on fruit, supplementing their diet with
occasional reptiles, small birds, or mammals.

LIFE IN THE TREES
Chameleons have
remarkable toes that are
specialized for life in the
trees. The toes are arranged
so the feet are able to clasp
branches securely while the tail
offers extra support, twisting and
twining itself around small twigs.
This Madagascan chameleon has a
sticky tipped tongue, which it is able
to shoot out further than the length of
its body, guaranteeing it a good diet of
insects and other small invertebrates.

In the outback

EUCALYPTUS EATER
The koala, *Phascolarctus cinereus*, is a marsupial and eats only the tough, leathery leaves of 12 species of eucalyptus gum tree. It is totally arboreal, only able to live in the trees because it has four hands to grip branches, and its feet are not suitable for walking.

AUSTRALIA IS HOME to some of the most extraordinary animals in the world. It has been an island continent for millions of years, and its wildlife has developed in a very individual way. There are over 150 kinds of pouched mammals, or marsupials, in Australia, and only 70 other such species in other parts of the world. Marsupials, including the largest the kangaroo, are born tiny, naked, and blind, and wriggle from the birth opening to a teat in the mother's pouch. They stay in the pouch, well-protected and feeding on the mother's milk, until they are large enough to survive outside. In the case of the kangaroo, when it is big enough, the young kangaroo, or joey, hops in and out of the pouch while its mother grazes. There are many other animals that are only found in Australia, including some of the most poisonous snakes in the world.

Large, broad bill to catch and swallow prey

Large head with brown ear patch

Warm fur

Laughing kookaburra
Dacelo novaeguineae

BIRD WITH A SENSE OF HUMOUR
The laughing kookaburra is named after its chuckling territorial calls, which are sometimes loud and booming, and sometimes quiet. It is a giant kingfisher that lives in the eastern half of Australia in family groups. The kookaburra has a very varied diet, pouncing on snakes, mammals, birds, and invertebrates. Despite the fact that it is a kingfisher, it only occasionally dives into water after fish. It is 41–46 cm (16–18 in) in length and has a large head and bill relative to its body size.

Stiff tail used as support

IN LEAPS AND BOUNDS
There are over 40 species in the kangaroo and wallaby family. There is no real difference between a kangaroo and a wallaby: larger species tend to be called kangaroos, and smaller ones wallabies. The family name is Macropodidae, which means "big feet", and they certainly do have big feet that they use to bound along in great leaps and bounds, while the tail acts as a counterbalance. Some large kangaroos can travel at 60 km/h (36 mph)! These marsupials are herbivorous, grazing on plants as they move along slowly, resting their heavy tails and front paws on the ground for balance and swinging the back legs forward.

White's tree frog
Litoria caerulea

Doria's tree kangaroo
*Dendrolagus
dorianus*

STICKY-TOED AMPHIBIAN
White's tree frog has round toe-pads
that are sticky with mucus. It lives in
forests, although it is familiar to many
Australians because it also lives in water
barrels and lavatories. It is 5–10 cm (2–4 in)
long and feeds on any moving creature
small enough to be swallowed. These frogs
spawn in water, producing 200 to 2,000 eggs.

Large ears

UP A TREE
Tree kangaroos have
evolved from ground-
living ancestors. They climb
trees to browse on foliage, but
most species can still hop over the
ground. Doria's tree kangaroo is the
most arboreal. It has strong forelegs,
broad hind feet, sharp claws, and can
no longer hop like other kangaroos.
This tree kangaroo lives in the cooler
forests of the New Guinea highlands
and has a thick fur coat to keep warm.

*Sharp
eyesight*

*Long tail acts as
counterbalance
when kangaroo
climbs trees*

*Powerful
shoulders*

*Powerful
claws*

*Deadly sting
in the tail*

*Hands used for
pulling down
vegetation and
sparring with
other males*

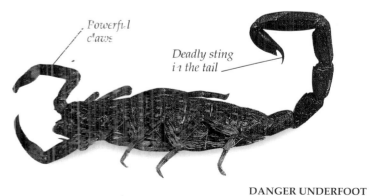

DANGER UNDERFOOT
There are many poisonous creatures to be found in the outback.
The marbled scorpion *Lychas marmoreus* lurks under bark and
among leaf litter, where it hunts for small invertebrates. These
are usually overpowered by the front claws and jaws. The
venomous sting in the tail is used primarily for defence.

Penguins of the Antarctic

THERE ARE 18 DIFFERENT SPECIES of penguin and they are all found south of the equator. Some live in cool waters off the coasts of New Zealand, southern Australia, and South Africa. Others live off the west coast of South America and in the Galápagos Islands in the Pacific. But the vast majority prefer to live in the far south, in the frozen seas and islands off the coast of Antarctica. These flightless birds divide their time between the sea and the land. They travel up to 800 km (500 miles) in the winter months in search of krill, fish, and squid to eat, returning to rookeries on land to breed during the warmer summer months. A penguin has a thick, waterproof coat, with short feathers which have oily tips that overlap and stop water soaking through. Underneath is a thick layer of down that traps the warm air given out by the penguin's body. There is also a layer of fat immediately under the skin which stops heat loss from the body.

KEEPING WARM
Emperor penguins are able to raise one chick a year because the female lays the egg in the depths of winter on the icy surface of the Antarctic continent. The male penguin then incubates the egg under a brood patch, or flap of skin. The resulting chick – this one is about eight weeks old – benefits from the same extra warmth and protection as it grows.

Incubating male Emperor penguins
Aptenodytes forsteri

Emperors often turn their backs on the constantly shifting wind

The birds in the centre are the warmest

Heat loss can be reduced by as much as 50 per cent

Birds take turns to occupy the most exposed positions

TOGETHERNESS
Incubating male Emperor penguins huddle together for warmth, moving very little to conserve energy. When the chicks are born, the birds still huddle together as much as possible. Some Emperor colonies contain over 20,000 pairs.

After the females return from fishing, the hungry males head for the open sea

Penguin "flies" out of water to draw breath

Penguin catches fish and krill in its beak

Penguin shoots onto land or ice in giant leap of up to 2 m (6.5 ft)

DUCKING AND DIVING
Over a long time, penguins' wings have evolved to form flippers with which they "fly" through the water. When they are swimming fast, they often use a technique called porpoising, leaping out of the water like dolphins or porpoises. Air offers less resistance to movement than water, so porpoising penguins can travel at speeds of up to 30 km/h (18 mph).

Under the water, penguin steers with its feet and tail

Bill is small to cut down on heat loss

King penguin
Aptenodytes patagonica

KING OF ALL THEY SURVEY

Nearly as big as an Emperor, at 1 m (3.3 ft) tall, the handsome King penguin breeds in huge colonies containing thousands and thousands of birds. It breeds on Antarctica and the sub-Antarctic islands, but relies on a warmer breeding climate than the Emperor, so it only raises on average two chicks every three years, and the chicks take 10 to 13 months to fledge. When the chick has hatched, the parent birds go on fishing trips that last between 4 and 8 days. The youngsters wait, huddled together in enormous crèches. The average weight of an adult King penguin is 15 kg (33 lb), so parents need to catch between 50 and 90 squid or fish each trip to the sea.

Penguin feeds chick by regurgitating catch

Overlapping, closely-packed feathers cover a thick layer of blubber

King penguins lay only one egg, carrying it around on their feet, covered by a brood patch

Small feet cut down on heat loss

Adaptable animals

To SURVIVE THE CONTRASTING SEASONS in some parts of the world, animals have to change too. As winter approaches, some mammals grow thick fur coats, which may be white for camouflage against the snow. They store a thick layer of fat in their skin to trap extra warmth and act as a food store in lean times. Birds also have layers of fat and dense, fluffy feathers to keep out the cold. For many birds and mammals, the severe winter weather is just too much. They migrate south to warmer places, returning again in spring. Insects rest in the warmer soil over the winter, usually in the form of larvae, and are able to withstand the freezing temperatures. As summer arrives, birds and mammals moult their thick coats. Animals that turn white in winter, turn brown for summer camouflage.

FINE FURS
People in cold countries always wore fur clothes to keep warm through the coldest winters. They usually obtained them by snaring their original owners in traps.

Arctic fox
Alopex lagopus

DRESSED FOR SUMMER
In summer, the Arctic fox grows a thinner coat of brownish-grey fur over most of its body. These colours match the brownish-grey rocks of the tundra landscape, making the fox hard to see, so that it can creep up on its prey, such as lemmings, without being spotted. The fox stores food under rocks during the summer and comes back to eat it in the winter months when food is hard to find. Arctic foxes have a varied diet, eating anything from berries, shells, and dead animals to garbage, birds, and eggs. But lemmings are vital to their diet and Arctic foxes endure weeks of starvation if there are few lemmings about.

The chest and belly are usually a pale grey-white in colour

Short legs lose less heat than long ones as there is less surface area exposed to the air

Thick, bushy tail can be curled around the body for warmth during blizzards or when resting or sleeping

Antarctic ice fish
Chaenocephalus aceratus

ANTI-FREEZE IN ITS VEINS
Many Antarctic fishes have anti-freeze molecules in their bodies which enable them to live in a "supercooled" state; their body fluids remain liquid at temperatures below the point at which ice forms. Antarctic ice fish (such as this one) have almost translucent blood.

Hair under paws stops fox sinking in snow; the fox's Latin name is Alopex lagopus – lagopus means "hairy foot"

Rock ptarmigan,
Lagopus mutus,
in summer plumage

Rock ptarmigan in
winter plumage

A BIRD FOR ALL SEASONS

Ptarmigans change their plumage twice a year, so that they are well camouflaged at all times. Their feather density also increases in winter. When resting overnight ptarmigans sometimes burrow in snow to reduce heat loss.

KEEPING WARM WITH FAT

Whales and seals are kept warm by a layer of thick fat called blubber. This fat walrus is in no danger of getting cold. Walruses can weigh up to 1,600 kg (1.8 tons), and have tusks 1 m (3.3 ft) long.

Dense fur coat with long hairs traps body warmth

Ears are furry inside and out for extra warmth

Small, round ears and a short muzzle cut down on heat loss; foxes from warmer places have larger ears and a longer muzzle

Sharp, pointed teeth to grab animals such as lemmings

DOUBLE-GLAZED FUR

The Arctic fox's white winter fur is made up of hairs which are hollow inside and full of air. The air in the hairs traps body warmth from the fox in much the same way as a double-glazed window traps warmth from houses. Air is a good insulator and does not let heat pass through it easily. The Arctic fox can tolerate temperatures of –40°C (–40°F), or even lower, quite comfortably.

Sharp claws used to dig through snow to find food

GIANT WEED
Similar species of coastal kelps are found around the world and many are very large indeed – some plants are tens of metres long. Waves and water currents pull on the enormous fronds with great force, so the kelp is fastened to the rocks of the shoreline by gnarled, root-like structures called holdfasts. These hold tight to the rock, like a tree's roots in the soil. Well-anchored kelp protects many ocean dwellers from the sun and lessens the force of waves and winds, so many smaller plants and shore animals such as crabs, fish, prawns, and molluscs, take advantage of the calmer conditions in the protective forests of kelp.

CHAPTER 5

LIFE IN THE WATER

IN THE FRESH WATERS of rivers and lakes, and the
salt waters of seas and oceans there is a multitude of
habitats. Water is a rich environment, teeming with life,
but tides, winds, waves, water currents, temperature,
and climate can make it a difficult one in which to live.

SHAGGY SHELLS
Gaping file shells, *Lima hians*, move
by expelling water from their shell
and using the mass of orange tentacles
like oars. They cannot withdraw the
tentacles inside the two halves
of the shell for protection,
so the tentacles produce
a sour-tasting, sticky
substance to deter
predators. Gaping file
shells build homes in
seaweed like this maerl,
a chalky, red seaweed
that grows along the
stony seabed.

Freshwater fish

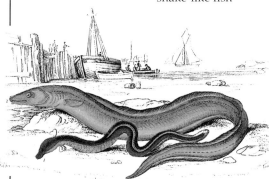

Eels are snake-like fish

MOST PEOPLE'S EXPERIENCE of freshwater fish are as dark torpedo shapes cruising silently below the surface of a river or pond. This ability to remain elusive has served freshwater fish well, and an amazing variety of species are supremely suited to underwater life. They swim by flexing powerful muscles that move the body to and fro. This produces a thrashing motion that propels the fish along. The fins are used chiefly for stabilizing, steering, and braking. The stripe along a fish's side is called the lateral line. It is a groove of specialized tissue that detects vibrations in the water, in effect allowing the fish to "hear" and "feel" water movements. Most of the fish on these two pages demonstrate a clever camouflage trick called countershading. Their back is dark and dull, so when viewed from above, they blend in with the murky water and the pond or river bed. The belly is shiny and silvery, so that when seen from below, the fish merges in with the ripples and flashes on the underside of the water's surface, thus avoiding predators.

Lateral line for detecting water movements

Roach has red iris

RUDD
This is a fish of still water, and the more weeds the better. The rudd can be distinguished from the roach (above right) by its fins: in the rudd, the front edge of the dorsal (back) fin is farther back than the base of the ventral (belly) fin, while in the roach these are in line. In some areas, rudd interbreed with roach or bream. Rudd can weigh about 2 kg (4.5 lb).

Rudd
Scardinius erythrophthalmus

Rudd has orange iris

Ventral fins are bright orange

Tench
Tinca tinca

Young roach

YOUNG ROACH
When they are young, fish are very difficult to identify. This one is probably a young roach and bears very little resemblance to the older roach shown above.

TENCH
Tiny scales, a greenish sheen, an almost unforked tail, and a bulky, muscular body are characteristics of this still-water, bottom-feeding member of the carp family. A good-sized tench weighs around 4 kg (9 lb), and the fish is a powerful fighter.

Short barbels

Medieval ailments were treated with slime from tench skin

Unforked tail

Dorsal fin in line with ventral fins

ROACH
The roach is a common fish that tolerates all kinds of conditions, from clear rivers to muddy, mildly polluted canals. It is not a fussy eater, and will take both plant and animal food. Roach are superficially similar to rudd (below left) and dace. They live for about ten years, and the largest grow to 2 kg (4.5 lb) in weight.

Roach
Rutilis rutilis

Salmon can leap 3 m (10 ft) over obstacles when travelling upriver

SALMON
The "king of fish" hatches in gravelly, fast-flowing water. It spends the first three or so years of its life in a river, and during this time is known as a "parr". It then migrates to the sea, becoming more silvery in colour and now known as a "smolt". After one to four years feeding in the sea, mature adults return to the river of their birth to spawn.

Dark spot on spiny dorsal fin

Perch
Perca fluviatilis

Grass carp
Ctenopharyngodon idella

GRASS CARP
This plant-eating, golden-coloured fish is a native of China and Russia, and has been introduced into many waterways to control weed growth. In its native habitat it can grow up to 35 kg (77 lb) in weight, although introduced specimens are usually around 4 kg (9 lb) in weight.

PERCH
The five or so dark vertical bars on the flanks, the two dorsal fins – the front one with prominent spines – and the reddish ventral and anal fins, mark out the perch as an exceptionally handsome fish. This youngster is one or two years old and may weigh 2 kg (4.5 lb) when fully grown. Perch feed on worms, crustaceans, molluscs, insects, and small fish.

Distinctive markings on tail

Dorsal fin

Mouth can be extended to suck up food from lake bottom

Barbels on side of mouth

Koi carp
Cyprinus carpio

Distinctive markings make these fish highly prized

KOI CARP
People in Japan and China have been breeding carp for hundreds of years. The koi is a cultivated variety of fish belonging to the same group as the common carp, and is known in Japan as Nishiki Koi, or "Brocaded carp". Kois have been bred for their colour and patterning as well as for size – some grow to over 1 m (3 ft) long. They have been stocked in ponds and lakes across Europe and North America, and prized specimens are extremely valuable.

Underwater weeds

Submerged weeds grow in ponds and rivers like trees in a miniature underwater forest. They provide shelter for some animals, and places of ambush for others from which to pounce on unwary victims swimming by. Underwater weeds are food for many creatures, from pond snails to ducks. They also provide that most vital substance, oxygen. As a plant carries out photosynthesis (pp. 40–41), it produces oxygen as a by-product. The oxygen diffuses into the water and is used by both plants and animals for the process of respiration. On a sunny day, small bubbles of oxygen coat the leaves of underwater plants, and occasionally rise to the surface of the water.

Rigid hornwort
*Ceratophyllum
demersum*

CURTAIN OF ROOTS
The water violet's roots hang like a veil in the water. The stem grows out of the water, where it bears not leaves but pale, pinky, five-petalled flowers.

*Developing
stem with flower*

Water violet
Hottonia palustris

TOTALLY SUBMERGED
The feathery-looking rigid hornworts are very much at home in the water. Even the flowers are submerged, growing at the junction of the leaf and the stem.

New Zealand
pygmyweed

TINY LARDER
This ball is volvox, a microscopic water plant, an important food for the tiny water creatures that inhabit ponds and rivers everywhere.

*Many-stranded
trailing roots*

Canadian
waterweed
*Elodea
canadensis*

SMALL PROBLEM
The underwater New Zealand pygmyweed is causing concern in many waterways because of its uncontrolled spread. It was first introduced as a aquarium oxygenator.

TRAVELLER
Canadian waterweed was carried from North America to Europe in about 1840, and soon colonized and clogged ponds and rivers there.

INVISIBLE TO THE EYE
At 25 x magnification,
the microscopic world
of underwater plants is
revealed. This drop of
pond water is teeming
with plankton.

PERCH IN THE GRASS
Tape grass is one of
the popularly named
"river grasses". It
provides a hideout
for many fish,
particularly the
perch, which is well
camouflaged with
the vertical stripes
it has on its sides.

Tape grass
*Vallisneria
spiralis*

*Narrow leaves
resemble needles
of a fir tree*

*Tall, grasslike
stems grow
close together*

Bulbous rush

SLENDER WATERWEED
The pale green water
starwort sways in large
clumps in the water.
Water starwort is a
favourite shelter
for the shy loach
which only emerges
to forage for food at
dusk.

RUSHED GROWTH
The bulbous rush is
usually rooted on the
pondside, but sometimes
it grows underwater,
becoming very
elongated.

Water
starwort
*Callitriche
stagnalis*

Floating flowers

The sacred lotus water-lily

I_N ANCIENT TIMES_ people saw that, when a previously dry watercourse filled with rains, the splendid blooms of water-lilies would soon appear. These aquatic plants gained a reputation as a symbol of immortality; the ancient Egyptians even worshipped one type of water-lily, the sacred lotus. The daily routine of their flowers makes water-lilies even more mysterious: they remain closed during the morning, open to reveal their beauty at around noon, and close again towards evening. This is in fact an adaptation to aid pollination by flying insects, which are more active when it is warm. The weather also affects whether the flowers will appear. On overcast days they may open only partially, but when wind or rain is imminent, the blooms remain tightly closed, protecting them from damage. Water-lilies grow in lakes, ponds, and slow-moving rivers. Their long, tough, rubbery stems are anchored to the muddy bed up to 3 m (10 ft) below.

NUISANCE OR FRIEND?
The flowering water hyacinth floats freely on the surface of the water carrying its roots below. It is borne along by the water currents and breezes, spreading rapidly and often clogging rivers and canals. However, the roots are good at trapping the harmful substances which pollute rivers and lakes. They are often planted in them by scientists to "strain" the water and clean them of toxins.

Waxy coating repels water droplets

Red hybrid – "Escarboucle"

Yellow water-lily leaves are patterned with a red tinge

Silky hairs cover surface of leaves, preventing them from becoming waterlogged and sinking under water

Leaves may be heart-shaped, oval, or round

Conspicuous yellow stamens

LILIES AND THEIR HYBRIDS

There are over 60 species of water-lilies around the world. In some areas they are known as lotuses. Their magnificent waxy-looking flowers and bold circular leaves have made them favourites for growing in ponds, ornamental water gardens, and landscaped lakes. A wide variety of different coloured flowers known as hybrids have been bred by horticulturalists.

Waxy petals

Yellow hybrid – "Chromatella"

FLOATING SAUCERS

The Amazonian water-lily has some of the largest leaves of any plant. A single leaf may be more than 1.5 m (5 ft) across, and has an upturned rim with reinforcing ribs beneath.

WATER LILY LEAF CASE

A caterpillar of the china mark moth cuts out an oval of leaf, fastening it to the underside with silk thread to form a protective case where it stays underwater until ready to emerge as a moth.

Water-lily leaf

WELL-USED LEAVES

The leaves, also known as "lily pads", are used by many creatures that live in the water. In the spring, pond snails lay their speckled, jelly-like egg masses on the undersides of lily pads. Frogs rest on or under them, waiting to snap up unwary insects. In places, the leaves grow so densely that some creatures can walk across them. The African jacana, a bird with long, widespread toes, is known as the "lily-trotter" as it steps delicately from pad to pad on its search for insects and seeds.

Waterfowl

WATER AND ITS RESIDENT wildlife attracts an amazing variety of birds. There are about 150 species of wildfowl, including swans, geese, and ducks, which are quite at home on the ponds, lakes, and rivers, as well as seashores of the world. These generally heavy-bodied birds have webbed feet for swimming, and long, mobile necks for dabbling in the water and rummaging in the muddy bed for food. During spring, the dense bank vegetation provides many species with safe and sheltered nesting sites. In summer, the proud parents can be seen leading their fluffy chicks across the surface of the water. Aquatic plants and animals are a ready source of food for most of the year. In winter, when ponds freeze over, many wildfowl retreat to parks and gardens where they feast on scraps donated by well-wishing humans. Others fly south, often covering vast distances to find a more favourable climate in which to spend the winter.

Nest and eggs of
eider duck
Somateria mollissima

*Soft down feathers
insulate eggs in nest*

Nest and eggs
of common teal

SPECIALLY GROWN DOWN
Ultra-soft eider-down feathers grow on the female eider duck's breast. She plucks them to cocoon her eggs as she nests on sea- or lakeshore, or on the river bank.

TEAL NEST
The teal makes its nest in dense undergrowth, using twigs and grasses. The female is very careful when visiting her chicks, so as not to attract predators.

TUFTED DUCK EGG
The six to fourteen eggs of the tufted duck are laid in a nest close to the water's edge. The chicks hatch after 25 days, and within a day are swimming.

Teal is one of the smallest ducks

ON THE WING
Pintails, like most ducks, can escape from danger with a twisting and turning flight. They open and close their pointed wings (right) to change direction. All wildfowl are strong fliers, many covering vast distances during an annual migration.

Pintail wing

MUTED COLOURS
Out of the breeding season, the pintail drake moults to the inconspicuous "eclipse" plumage, which resembles the female's colours.

PLUMAGE
In the breeding season, most male ducks, like the pintail (far right) sport bright plumage to catch the eye of the female. The female (right) is a duller colour, for camouflage on the nest.

TUFTED DUCK FOOD
The tufted duck feeds on freshwater mussels, as well as small fish, frogs, and any insects it can catch.

Tufted duck
Aythya fuligula

Tufted duck skull

MUSCOVY DUCK BILL
This native of Central and South American ponds and marshes has a broad bill with which it feeds on aquatic plants and animals alike.

Muscovy duck
Cairina moschata

Muscovy duck skull

MUTE SWAN THREAT
The mute swan's bill (below) is normally covered by an orange sheath. Male swans can be extremely vicious, particularly in the breeding season, when defending territory.

Mute swan
Cygnus olor

Broad bill of swan suitable for dabbling for water vegetation

Mute swan skull

Outer vane (windward edge of feather)

Flight feathers

Long quill

FEATHER CARE
Water-dwelling birds depend on feathers to stay dry. They spend a lot of time preening their feathers to keep them in good condition and rid them of parasites.

River life

FROM THE COLD, RUSHING WATERS of mountain streams to the warm, sluggish coastal swamps of the tropics, the rivers of the world are home to a wealth of wildlife. The rainwater that falls on mountaintops and forms the streams is chemically pure, but as it travels down towards the sea, it gradually collects particles and dissolved nutrients from the rocks and plants over which it rushes, becoming warmer and oxygenated and able to sustain animal life. Rivers and streams are very rich in wildlife. Plants take root in the soft, damp soil of the river bank, and animals dig burrows. Crustaceans, amphibians, and fish eat insect larvae under water, while the adult insects mate and feed above the surface. In turn, these flying insects are eagerly snapped up by hungry birds and bats.

Grey wagtail
Motacilla cinerea

BUSY BIRD
The grey wagtail snaps up flies, midges, small dragonflies, and water beetles with its long beak. It often catches insects when in flight.

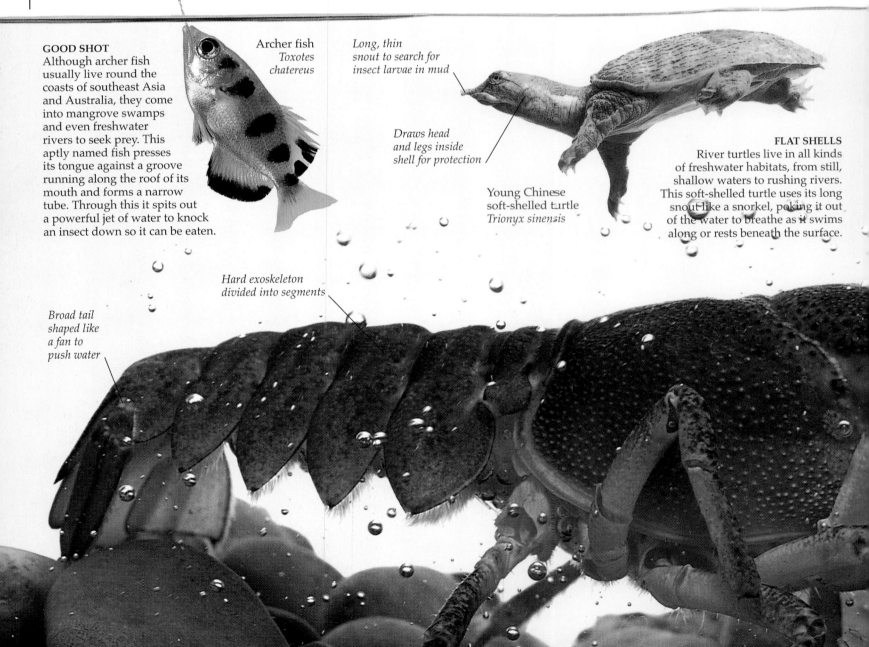

GOOD SHOT
Although archer fish usually live round the coasts of southeast Asia and Australia, they come into mangrove swamps and even freshwater rivers to seek prey. This aptly named fish presses its tongue against a groove running along the roof of its mouth and forms a narrow tube. Through this it spits out a powerful jet of water to knock an insect down so it can be eaten.

Archer fish
Toxotes chatereus

Long, thin snout to search for insect larvae in mud

Draws head and legs inside shell for protection

Young Chinese soft-shelled turtle
Trionyx sinensis

FLAT SHELLS
River turtles live in all kinds of freshwater habitats, from still, shallow waters to rushing rivers. This soft-shelled turtle uses its long snout like a snorkel, poking it out of the water to breathe as it swims along or rests beneath the surface.

Hard exoskeleton divided into segments

Broad tail shaped like a fan to push water

WATERSIDE SNAKE

The viperine water snake is well suited to a watery life. It can swim easily across the surface of the water bending its streamlined body from side to side like an eel. It mainly eats fish, but sometimes takes frogs, worms, newts, and toads. It spends a lot of time in the water, but comes out on land to bask in the sun, as well as to hibernate in winter.

Wagtail gets its name from habit of wagging tail up and down when it lands on a rock or branch

WATERSIDE PLANT

The long, branched roots of the common alder stop the muddy soil of the river bank from being washed away by swirling currents. In turn, the ripe cones of the alder drop their seeds into the river, where they are carried along by the water to new stretches of the river bank.

Young viperine
water snake
Natrix maura

Common alder
Alnus glutinosa

CREATURE OF THE RIVER BED

The crayfish lives in lakes and rivers, but can only survive if the water is clean. It is a close relative of the sea-dwelling lobster, and like it has a protective outer skin, known as the exoskeleton. This exoskeleton will not stretch, so the crayfish sheds it every so often in order to grow. While it is waiting for its soft new skin to harden, the vulnerable crayfish hides from predators. The first pair of legs are larger than the others, forming pincers called chelipeds. The males mainly use their chelipeds for defence and to hold on to the female during mating.

Alder cones

European crayfish
Austropotamobius pallipes

Minnow
Motacilla cinerea

Joint allows legs to bend for walking

Long antennae to help find food

FRESHWATER FISH

Minnows live in clear, fast-flowing rivers and streams, sheltering in quiet pools close to the river banks. They feed mainly on water insects and other water creatures, pushing their jaws forward to take their prey. They often swim together in large groups, and their bodies are streamlined to help them swim fast to escape predators.

The salt marsh

MANY ESTUARIES throughout the world are flanked by a broad expanse of land, riddled with creeks and channels, the salty soil supporting its own, very distinctive, plant population. This is the salt marsh, and it is a very forbidding habitat for plants. Twice each day, sea water soaks into the soil and mud. As the tide retreats, evaporation leaves behind a salty residue. Spring tides flood the entire marsh with seawater. Yet a few hours later, at low tide, heavy rain may have turned the surface into an almost freshwater habitat. The plants growing on a salt marsh have specially adapted to such fluctuating conditions.

PINKS AND PURPLES
Many marsh plants have pink, lavender, or purple flowers, colouring the whole marsh when in bloom. They tend to flower late in summer or in autumn.

Flowerspike

Flowerhead

MARSH GRASS
The flowerheads of couch grass show in this clump of grasses from the higher, drier part of the marsh.

Sea aster
Aster tripolium

PLAIN PLANTAIN
The inconspicuous sea plantain populates the flat expanses of the salt marshes.

SEA ASTER
In late summer and early autumn, the distinctive purple and yellow flowers of sea aster carpet large areas of the salt marsh.

Flower stalk rising out of clump of fleshy leaves

Sea plantain
Plantago maritima

Flower-spike

SEA-LAVENDER
In late summer, the flowers of the sea-lavender turn the salt marsh lilac.

Couch grass
Agropyron repens

Leaves have a bluish tinge

SEA ARROW GRASS
Among the dry, grassy stems of the marsh, there are the fleshy stems of sea arrow grass. Despite its name, it is not a true grass.

Sea-lavender
Limonium vulgare

Sea arrow grass family
Gramineae

SEA PURSLANE
The silvery-green leaves of the sea purslane are covered with minute air-filled protective scales. Sea purslane grows along the edges of the channels and creeks within the salt marsh.

Ripening seed heads

Sea purslane
Halimione portulacoides

Leaves take up or lose water as salinity changes

ANNUAL SEABLITE
The thick, fleshy leaves of this annual seablite are typical of many plants of the salt marsh. The succulent leaves store water until it is needed.

BINDING IN THE MARSH
Cord grass, an early colonizer of bare mud, is often planted on the lower parts of marshes and estuaries, to stabilize the ground with its underground stems and thick root system.

RICH PICKINGS
Knots and many other wading birds probe the mud of the salt marsh channels for plants and insects.

Cord grass
Spartina anglica

Glasswort
Salicornia europaea

Annual seablite
Suaeda maritima

The leaves secrete salt crystals to rid the plant of excess salt

Swollen, jointed stems store water

SALT MARSH STABILIZER
Glasswort is one of the first plants to colonize the estuary mud, its delicate roots beginning the stabilizing process.

Thick roots supply plant with nutrients

TIDAL DEBRIS
Each tide sweeps old stems, bits of crab, and other sundry debris along the water channels that riddle the marsh.

Crabs

CAST-UP REMAINS
Young shore crabs and cockles, and a whelk's spongy, empty egg case are some of the items found when "marsh-combing" along the channel edges.

MARSH MUD
Squelching, oozing mud, rich in organic matter, is the stuff of life in the salt marsh and estuary.

Empty shells

Roots bind the slippery mud

Whelk egg case

Swamp life

DEEP LAYERS of mud and silt accumulate along sheltered tropical coastlines and in river estuaries. A number of different kinds of trees colonize these areas of still or slow-moving water. They are collectively known as mangroves and form swampy forests. Mangroves are the only trees that can live in the salt water that is carried in and out of the swamp by the tide twice a day. Among the tangled roots of the mangroves live an amazing variety of animals that have adapted to the tidal ebb and flow of these thick jungles. Snapping turtles feed on water plants and carrion, while fiddler crabs emerge from muddy burrows to gather food. Water lettuces and water hyacinths provide food for the hungry plant-eaters, while overhead, iguanas and mangrove snakes sun themselves in the leafy branches.

IN THE TREES
The leafy canopy above the still waters of the swamp is home to many different animals. This agile green iguana is only 15 cm (6 in) long and lives in the swamps of the Caribbean, Central America, and South America. It is active during the day, sunbathing in leafy mangrove branches and leaping into the water if threatened. This fruit- and leaf-eating reptile has long, well-spread toes with sharp claws for gripping branches and twigs. Its scaly skin protects it and also stops it drying out.

No teeth, but hard, sharp edge to mouth

Water lettuce
Pistia stratiotes

FIERCE SNAPPER
The snapping turtle lives in the still, warm waters of swamps and creeks. It is slow-moving, but well protected by its 8-cm (3-in) long shell and it has a fierce bite. The turtle spends most of its time in shallow water, well camouflaged among the floating plants, waiting for fish or other prey to swim past. Its feet are adapted for moving both under water and on land. To get about in the water, it usually walks on the bottom, using its claws to grip the mud or rocks.

FLOATING PLANT
Water lettuces float on the surface, their roots in the water. The waterproof leaves have air-filled floats that keep them the right way up. The leaves are broad and flat to absorb the sunlight the plant used to produce its food.

Trailing roots absorb nutrients from the water

Strong legs with webbed toes and long claws

FIDDLER CRABS
As the tide recedes and the tangle of roots and mud is revealed, fiddler crabs pop out of their burrows and scuttle about looking for particles of food, such as algae, on the surface of the mud. Fiddlers have one giant pincer which they use to signal to females, and to scare away other males. They are fiercely territorial, and usually simply threaten another male by waving the claw in the air. However, they will, on occasion, lock claws, until one fiddler gains dominance, and the other retreats. When the crabs are startled, they are able to run sideways very fast.

ADAPTED ROOTS
Other trees have formed specially adapted root systems to exist in difficult terrain. The palm *Verschaffeltia splendida* is found naturally only in the rainforests of the Seychelles Islands. It either grows in the wet conditions of the river valley bottoms or on the steep hillsides. The wet, rocky ground has a thin layer of soil and the thick stilt roots grow out from the lower part of the trunk. The stilt roots give the palm firm anchorage in watery soil.

*Fine hairs
help protect
trunk*

*New stilt root
grows out
from trunk*

*Splayed-out stilt
roots improve
anchorage in
mud*

MANGROVES

The mud and warm shallow seawater on tropical coastlines are very low in oxygen. So that their roots can breathe, mangroves have pneumatophores, roots that stick up above the mud and take in the air through large pores, or lenticels. The roots of this mangrove, *Rhizophora*, grow in a tangle of arches.

*Crab's eyes on
long stalks so they
can watch for danger*

Fiddler crab
Uca vocans

Inside a rock pool

A ROCK POOL is a natural world in miniature – a specialized habitat in which plants and animals live together. There is usually a wide range of plants, from the film of microscopic algae coating almost any bare surface, to wracks, and other large seaweeds. These plants capture light energy from the sun (pp. 12–13) and obtain nutrients from the seawater. The plants in turn provide food for winkles, limpets, and other plant-eaters. Flesh-eating animals, such as starfish, small fish, whelks, and other creatures eat the plant-eaters. Rock pool scavengers, such as crabs and prawns, eat both plant and animal material.

Toothed wrack
Fucus serratus

Velvet swimming crab
Macropipus puber

Blenny
Blennius pholis

Painted topshell
Calliostoma zizyphinum

LARGE FAMILY
There are about 1,500 species in the goby family, most of them small, flat, shore-dwellers. The spotted patterning helps conceal them in the shadows of the rock pool. These are sand gobies, which also immerse themselves in the sand to hide from predators.

VELVET SWIMMING CRAB
The velvet swiming crab sorts through settled debris at the bottom of the rock pool for food. Under the shell, two large chambers on either side of the main organs house the crab's gills, with which this crustacean absorbs the oxygen dissolved in seawater.

Sand gobies
Pornato schistus minutus

Open beadlet anemone
Actinia equina

Cushion star
Asterina gibbosa

CUSHION STARS
Like their larger cousins, the small cushion stars, or "starlets", are carnivorous (meat-eating). They devour little molluscs, brittlestars, and shore worms.

CLINGING TO THE ROCKS

Many of the animals found in rock pools are gastropods (snail-like molluscs), and they are all very good at clinging to the sides of rock pools. The common limpet can only be prised away if taken by surprise, before its muscular foot cements it to the rock. Winkles, topshells, conches, cowries, cone shells, and whelks all patrol the shoreline looking for food.

ANEMONES

When they are immersed in water, anemones protect themselves with tiny stinging cells in their tentacles. They also use these stinging cells to paralyse prey. However, when the tide retreats, this gem anemone folds in its 48 tentacles, as they cannot feed when the tide is out and this stops them drying out.

Red dulse seaweed
Rhodymenia
palmata

Edible periwinkle
Littorina littorea

Common limpet
Patella vulgata

Common prawn
Palaemon serratus

SHRIMP OR PRAWN?

These ten-limbed crustaceans look very similar. In general, shrimps have fatter bodies, blunt claws on only the first pair of limbs, and they live mostly in sand. Prawns (shown here) are thinner-bodied, have small, narrow pincers on the first two pairs of limbs, and live in pools and among seaweed.

Breadcrumb sponge
Halichondria panicea

BREADCRUMB SPONGE

Attached to the rock is a deep green sponge, the common breadcrumb sponge that is often found in shady gulleys and under boulders on the lower shore. Sponges are primitive animals that draw in water from which they extract oxygen and floating particles of food.

Snakelocks anemone
Anemonia sulcata

Common prawn
Palaemon serratus

Waders

IN THE SODA LAKES OF AFRICA'S GREAT RIFT VALLEY, flamingos flock in their hundreds of thousands, a sea of deep pink. They owe their colour to the pink pigment in the small shrimps that they sift and eat from the bottom mud. Flamingos nest on the ground in large colonies, the adults flying away every day to find more food and water. The long legs of the flamingos allow them to wade in deep water in their search for food. Where rivers meet the sea, the shallow, muddy waters of estuaries teem with a wealth of food, and these are rich waters for other long-legged wading birds, such as stilts, dunlins, and oystercatchers.

Large bill

Flamingos feed their young on a rich "milk" produced in the crop, part of the oesophagus

Lesser flamingo
Phoenicopterus minor

The more shrimps the flamingo eats the pinker the feathers become

Long neck

Slender bill

Long legs to wade through deep water while feeding

ESTUARY BIRD
The black-necked stilt lives in North America and northern South America, breeding in colonies on marshy ground or on the bare mud of the salt pans. In flight, their legs stick out 18 cm (7 in) beyond the tail to counterbalance the long neck and the weight of the head. The very long legs allow the stilt to feed on small creatures that it takes from the mud in deep water on shores and estuaries.

Black-necked stilt
Himantopus mexicanus

LONG LEGS
The long legs of the flamingo enable it to reach deep water, helping it to avoid competition for the available food from other, shorter-legged birds. Like ducks and geese, flamingos have webs of skin between their toes. The webs work like paddles when the bird is in water. They are also useful when the flamingo is walking on soft, marshy ground, as they spread the flamingo's weight evenly over the boggy surface.

148

Marabou stork
Leptoptilos crumeniferus

Characteristic hunched shoulders

Long bill for seizing prey

Adult has large throat pouch for inflation in courtship rituals

Flexible neck

Lesser flamingos are the smallest of the six species of flamingo

Marabou has longest legs of any stork

Sievelike edges on top bill to filter food

LARGE SCAVENGER
The Marabou stork of east Africa scavenges from the carcasses of large grazing animals and human rubbish tips. It also feeds on fish and frogs which it takes while wading in the shallow waters of river beds, and sometimes takes sick or injured birds and flamingo eggs and chicks. The Marabou stork is also called the "adjutant" or "adjutant stork" because of its extraordinary hunched military bearing. It is the largest species of stork, growing to a height of 1.5 m (5 ft).

FILTER FEEDING
The flamingo has a unique method of feeding. Sieve-like edges on its top bill filter out tiny plants and invertebrates from the surface of the water. The bottom bill and tongue move up and down to pump water through comb-like fringes on the sides of the top bill.

Large, splayed feet

Weather by the sea

THE PRESENCE OF SO MUCH WATER gives weather by the sea its own particular characteristics. Winds blowing in off the sea naturally carry more moisture than those blowing off the land, so coastal areas tend to be noticeably wetter than inland areas – especially if they face into the wind. They can be cloudier, too. Cumulus clouds, for instance, usually form inland only during the day, but on coasts facing the wind, they drift overhead at night as well, when cold winds blow in over the warm sea. Sometimes these clouds bring localized showers to coastal areas. Fogs too can form at sea in the same way, and creep a little way inland. At daybreak the sea is often shrouded in a thick mist that disperses only as the wind changes or as the sun's heat begins to dry the atmosphere. The overall effect of all this water is to make weather in coastal areas generally less extreme than farther inland. Because the sea retains heat well, nights tend to be warmer on the coast, with winters milder, and summers slightly cooler. Frosts are rare on sea coasts in the mid-latitudes.

OUT FOR A BLOW
Seaside resorts are often very windy, as depicted by this early 20th-century postcard. The open sea provides no obstacle to winds blowing off the sea, and temperature differences between land and sea can generate stiff breezes as well.

CLEAR COAST
This picture shows the coast of Oregon, but it is typical of west coasts everywhere in the mid-latitudes. Deep depressions are common at this latitude, and here a cold front has just passed over, moving inland. An overhang of cloud lingers in the upper air from the front itself, and cumulus clouds are still growing in its wake. More showers are clearly on the way. As the front moves inland, it may well produce progressively less rain, because there is less moisture available to feed its progress.

COASTAL FOG
Sea fog is an advection fog, which means that it occurs where a warm, moist wind blows over a cooler surface. Sea fog often happens off the coast of Newfoundland in Canada (left), where warm westerly winds blow over a sea cooled by currents flowing down from the Arctic. Sometimes thick fogs linger there for days on end.

1000 mb   A little cloud cover   Strong wind

WIND AND WAVES

The winds that help windsurfers skim across the surface of the sea often may be locally generated sea breezes. But the waves they ride may be created by winds thousands of kilometres away. Waves are whipped up by the wind when air turbulence over the water creates little pockets of low and high pressure that suck and push on the water. Just how big the waves are depends on the strength of the wind, how long it blows, and the "fetch" – that is, how far it blows over the water.

Nighttime land breeze

Warmer air from over sea pushes cool air over land downwards

Land cools quickly

Sinking air over land drives air seawards creating land breeze

Sea cools slowly

Air rising over warm sea pushes air at high altitude towards land

Daytime sea breeze

Air sinks over the cool sea

Air pushed out to sea at high altitude increases air pressure over cool sea

Air rises over warm land about 1 km (0.6 mile) over ground

Land warms up quickly in the warmth of the sun

Sea warms up only slowly

Sea air driven shorewards, creating stiff sea breeze at surface

Land and sea breezes

A marked characteristic of coastal areas is the frequent occurrence of land and sea breezes. Both occur because land and water absorb and lose heat from the sun at different rates. During the day, the land heats far more quickly than the sea, and air begins to rise. As warm air rises above the land, cool air from the sea is drawn in underneath, creating a stiff sea breeze, blowing inland. At night, the situation is reversed. The land cools more quickly, and air begins to sink. The cool air pushes out under the warm air over the sea. This is called a land breeze.

Turtles and tortoises

REPTILES WITH SHELLS, chelonians, are found in most warm parts of the world. There are over 250 species, and they live in salt water, freshwater, and on land. Marine chelonians are called turtles, and the rest are tortoises, but sometimes pond and river dwellers are known as terrapins. All chelonians lay eggs on land – some in sand, some in leaf litter, and some in the burrows of other animals. These reptiles have short, broad bodies, enclosed in a bony shell. The bone of the shell is usually covered by horny plates or, less commonly, by leathery skin. Chelonians are divided into two main groups according to the way the neck bends when the head retreats into the shell. Hidden-necked chelonians include terrapins, sea turtles, softshell turtles, and tortoises. Side-necked chelonians include the matamata and African mud turtles.

ALLIGATOR SNAPPING TURTLE
This turtle is ferocious both in appearance and its habits. It spends nearly all its time in water, lying motionless on the river bed, its mouth wide open, its knife-like jaws ready to scythe through its prey.

MIGRATING TURTLE
Some marine turtles have developed incredible migratory habits, travelling hundreds of kilometres from their feeding grounds to lay their eggs on the beaches where they were born. The green turtle travels to its nesting ground every two or three years.

Green turtle
Chelonia mydas

Turtles are air breathers, so must come to the surface regularly

LEATHER SHELLED
The largest of all turtles, this giant leatherback has a leathery, ridged skin above and below its body, instead of the usual horny plates. It usually lives in the mid-depths of the ocean waters, breeding in the warm waters of the Caribbean.

RED-EARED TERRAPIN
These chelonians get their names from the broad, red stripe that runs along the side of the head. Because they are gentle and attractive creatures, they are very popular as pets. Found in North America, they live in ponds and rivers, but frequently climb out of the water to bask, often on logs which they pile up several deep.

Red-eared terrapin
Pseudemys scripta elegans

HERMANN'S TORTOISE
Different life-styles lead to alterations in shell structure. Very few land tortoises have the speed or agility to escape a predator, so they usually have high-domed or knobbly shells as a defence against the predator's strong jaws. Turtles tend to have flatter shells which are streamlined for easy movement through the water. The soft-shelled tortoises have the flattest shells, to allow them to hide easily beneath sand and mud.

Hermann's tortoise
Testudo hermanni

High-domed shell

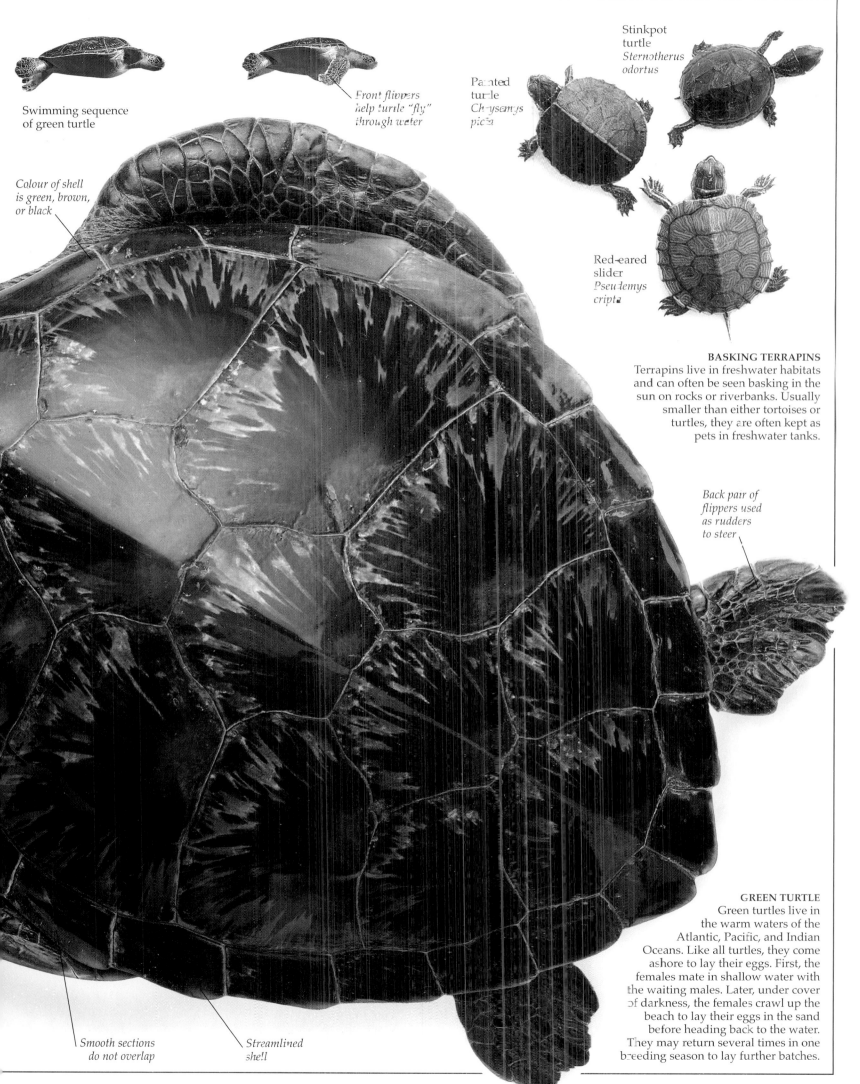

Swimming sequence
of green turtle

*Front flippers
help turtle "fly"
through water*

*Colour of shell
is green, brown,
or black*

Stinkpot
turtle
*Sternotherus
odortus*

Painted
turtle
*Chrysemys
picta*

Red-eared
slider
*Pseudemys
cripta*

BASKING TERRAPINS
Terrapins live in freshwater habitats
and can often be seen basking in the
sun on rocks or riverbanks. Usually
smaller than either tortoises or
turtles, they are often kept as
pets in freshwater tanks.

*Back pair of
flippers used
as rudders
to steer*

*Smooth sections
do not overlap*

*Streamlined
shell*

GREEN TURTLE
Green turtles live in
the warm waters of the
Atlantic, Pacific, and Indian
Oceans. Like all turtles, they come
ashore to lay their eggs. First, the
females mate in shallow water with
the waiting males. Later, under cover
of darkness, the females crawl up the
beach to lay their eggs in the sand
before heading back to the water.
They may return several times in one
breeding season to lay further batches.

Life on the rocks

ROCKY SHORES provide a diverse and complex environment for many types of marine creatures. The types of rocks from which a beach is made, its position in relation to the sea, and the range of tide levels all play a part in determining the variety of creatures that live there.

The tide may expose the rocky shore for several hours each day, and some creatures have built up a tolerance to living without water for extended periods. Those that do not manage to reach deeper waters, or find tidal pools when the water recedes, will dry out and die from exposure to the air and sun. The pounding of powerful waves erodes the rocks themselves. Many animals living there have evolved very strong shells that can withstand the force of the waves, and many have developed ways of anchoring themselves firmly to the surface of the rocks, so they are not washed away.

ROCK POOLS
Life can be hard in the shallow water pools left by receding tides. Many creatures that prefer less light and warmth are left stranded and must try their best to find shelter.

New Zealand mussel family
Mytilacea

Bearded ark shell family
Arcacea

BOUVIER'S CRAB
Like many small crabs, this one lives between or under rocks, and only emerges to scavenge for food at night.

BEARDED ARK SHELL
This bivalve gets its name from the tiny hairs that cover it. It lives in rock crevices, and attaches itself by means of a broad byssus. The shell often gets distorted as it grows to fit snugly into its rocky niche.

Mussel with byssal threads

Tail fan

Common blue mussels
Mytilus edulis

ANCHORED
Mussels are common inhabitants of many rocky shores, often living in massive clusters high on the shore. Mussels anchor themselves to rocks and other surfaces by means of byssal threads – strong, thin filaments secreted by a gland in the mussel's foot.

JEWEL IN A SHELL

This rough star-shell lives on the rocky shores of the Mediterranean, but is found below tide level. The shell is often encrusted with marine growths. The bright red operculum is sometimes used to make jewellery.

Operculum

WINKLES ON THE WEEDS

The tiny periwinkles are among the most common inhabitants of rocky shores. They tend to live high up on the shore, where they cling to the rocks and clumps of seaweed.

Rough periwinkles
Littorina saxatilis

Left large pincer or cheliped is larger and stronger than right

Antenna

Common shore crab

Antennule

Eyes tucked in under carapace

SHORE CRAB

The shore crab is one of the most common European crabs, and is often found lurking under rocks and seaweed on the seashore.

ELUSIVE LOBSTER

The common lobster is highly prized as a food, and is a favourite catch for divers. Lobsters can be difficult to find as they blend in well with their surroundings, and often hide in crevices during the day, with only their claws and antennae showing.

One of four pairs of walking legs

STONY-SHELLED CRAB

The Mediterranean stone crab is so called because of its heavy-looking, irregular shell.

Clever disguises

A CASUAL GLANCE into a rock pool may reveal only a few strands of seaweed and some dead-looking shells. But wait patiently, sitting low and still to avoid being seen, and watch carefully. A dark patch of rock may suddenly glide forward: it is a blenny, on the look-out for food. A slightly hazy-looking area of sand walks away: it is a prawn, adjusting the spots and lines on its body to blend perfectly with the background. A small pebble slides off: it is a winkle grazing on algae. A patch of gravelly bottom ripples and two eyes appear: a flatfish has wafted small pebbles and shell fragments over its body to break up its outline. All these creatures use camouflage to help conceal themselves from voracious predators and to catch prey themselves.

PALE UNDERSIDE
Flatfish are well camouflaged when viewed from the surface of the water. The underside, flat against the seabed, has no need of special colouring, so it is white or pale in many flatfish species.

WEED LOOKALIKE
The leafy sea-dragon, from the coastal waters of southern Australia, is a type of seahorse. Its loose lobes of skin resemble the seaweed fronds in which it hides.

Urchins graze the rocks and weeds, eating small algal growths and animals

URCHIN COVER-UP
Several species of sea-urchins grasp pebbles, shells, and pieces of seaweed with their long "tube feet" and hold them over their bodies. A well-draped urchin can be difficult to spot. These are green sea-urchins, which are found on the lower shore and in inshore waters.

Dab larvae move to depths of up to 70 m (230 ft) before becoming "flat"

A DAB HAND
Many flatfish can change colour to match the surface on which they are resting. Some minutes earlier, this young dab was a light sandy colour. It became several shades darker when placed on selected dark pebbles, the marks on its upper side becoming almost black. The largest dabs reach about 40 cm (16 in) in length.

*Eyes are both on
right side of face*

*Spots change
colour to blend
in with background*

HIDING PLAICE
The plaice is an expert at
camouflage, becoming almost
invisible on multi-coloured gravel.
It lives near the shore for the first few
years of its life, and then migrates to deeper
water. It may grow up to 60 cm (2 ft) in length.

BEING A BOULDER
This young edible crab has backed its way
into a group of like-coloured pebbles and is
now pretending to be a boulder. It remains
motionless with its pincers tucked under its
body. The scalloped edge of its carapace
(shell) gives
it away.

DEADLY STONE
The shallow waters of Pacific shores can
be a death-trap to the unwary. A stonefish,
which resembles a gnarled lump of
rocky coral, may suddenly erect
the deadly spines on its back
if trodden on. Its poison
can be fatal to humans.

Stonefish
Synanceja verrucosa

STEADY AS A ROCK
Resembling your surroundings
will only work as camouflage if
you stay very still like them, or move
as they move. Small fish like the butterfly
blenny (below) stay motionless on the rocks
for long periods, only
darting off to
chase prey
or avoid
predators.

Many-coloured seaweeds

THE MOST OBVIOUS seaweeds on the shore are usually the large brown seaweeds known as wracks and kelps. Wracks are leathery, strap-like seaweeds that grow in bands between the high- and low-tide marks. Some species have air bladders that keep the main body (the thallus) of the weed afloat as the waves come and go. The kelps have broader, blade-like fronds and usually live below the low-water mark. Red seaweeds are generally smaller and prefer rock pools and deeper water beyond the kelp zone. They contain a red pigment that masks out the green pigment chlorophyll, present in all plants. Red pigment uses the dim light that filters through the seawater much more efficiently than the dark pigment of brown seaweeds, so the red seaweeds are able to grow at greater depths.

Mature bladder wrack

Air pocket

FROM HIGH TO LOW
On rocky shores, seaweeds are found in horizontal bands or zones. These bands of bright-green seaweeds, greenish-brown wracks, red seaweeds, and brown kelps at the low-tide mark form a basic pattern which is repeated, with variations in the species, all over the world.

Serrated wrack
Fucus serratus

Immature bladder wrack
Fucus vesiculosus

POCKETS OF AIR
Some specimens of bladder wrack develop large air pockets in pairs along the central midrib of the frond (above right). Yet other specimens, especially on exposed coasts, have few or even no bladders. No one knows why this is so. A mature bladder wrack (as in the engraving above) has swollen tips that contain reproductive organs.

Sea lettuce
Ulva lactuca

FROM HIGH TO LOW
Sea lettuce (left and above), which looks a lot like the plant we eat in salads, can grow in many different habitats – in the slightly salty water of estuaries, in seawater, and even in mildly polluted waters. This green seaweed is very common. It can be found attached to rocks, floating freely, or washed up on shore.

WEED WITH TEETH
Toothed, or serrated, wrack is named after the saw-like teeth along the edges of its fronds. It is a member of the *Fucus* group, but unlike its close relatives, it has no air bladders.

A TASTY DISH
The two red seaweeds carragheen (right) and dulse (far right) are both red seaweeds that are harvested commercially. Carragheen provides a gel for making jellies and aspic as well as ice cream, while dulse can be eaten raw, cooked as a vegetable, or added to a stew or soup.

SUGAR AMONG THE SALT

The sugar kelp or sugar wrack is a big brown seaweed of the low-water level and below. Its crinkly fronds and wavy edges are distinctive, as is the sweet taste of the white powder that forms on its drying surface. It is eaten as a delicacy in the Far East.

LONG THONGS

Thongweed is a leathery, strap-like brown seaweed found near the low-water level. Its narrow fronds may grow more than 3 m (10 ft) long. Like many seaweeds, its tough and rubbery texture protects it from the pounding of the waves on the rocks.

Sugar kelp
Laminaria saccharina

Thongweed

BUTTON-SHAPED BASE

The button- or mushroom-shaped base is one stage in the life cycle of the thongweed. In the plant's second year of growth, the thongs develop from this base and contain the reproductive structures.

Nutrients are absorbed through the whole surface of the seaweed

Holdfasts (root-like structures) anchor brown seaweeds to rocks

Carragheen
Chondrus crispus

Dulse

Oceans of the world

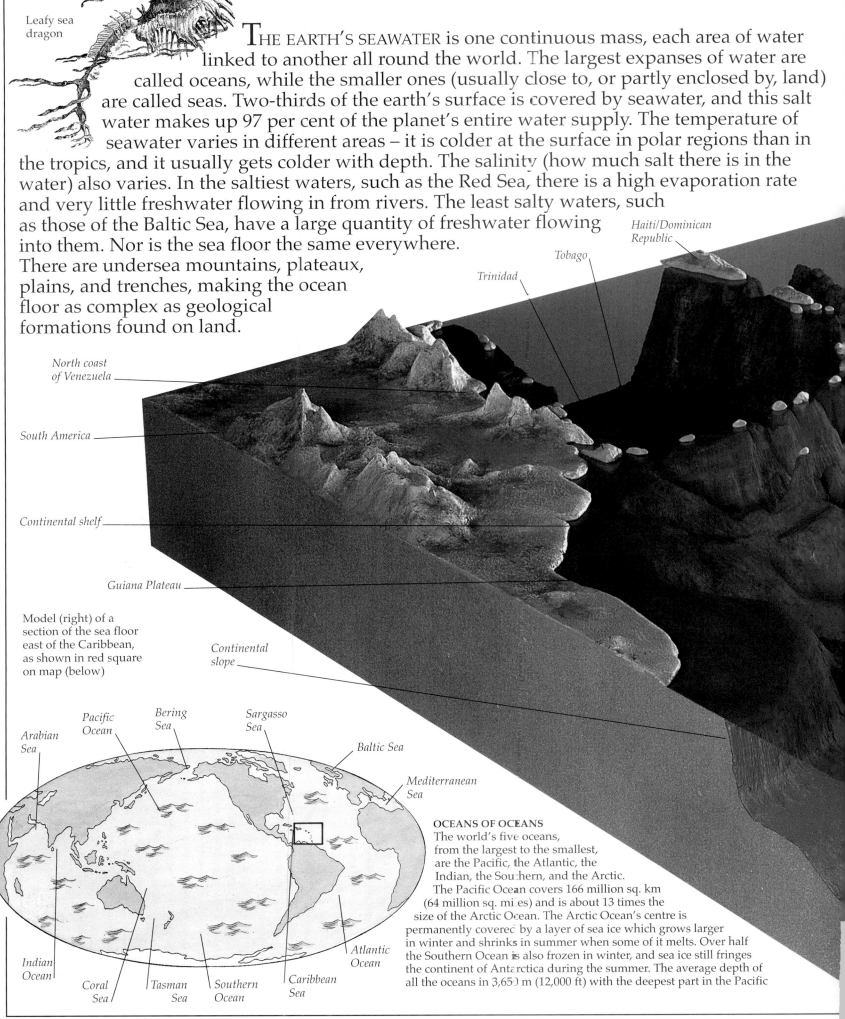

Leafy sea dragon

THE EARTH'S SEAWATER is one continuous mass, each area of water linked to another all round the world. The largest expanses of water are called oceans, while the smaller ones (usually close to, or partly enclosed by, land) are called seas. Two-thirds of the earth's surface is covered by seawater, and this salt water makes up 97 per cent of the planet's entire water supply. The temperature of seawater varies in different areas – it is colder at the surface in polar regions than in the tropics, and it usually gets colder with depth. The salinity (how much salt there is in the water) also varies. In the saltiest waters, such as the Red Sea, there is a high evaporation rate and very little freshwater flowing in from rivers. The least salty waters, such as those of the Baltic Sea, have a large quantity of freshwater flowing into them. Nor is the sea floor the same everywhere. There are undersea mountains, plateaux, plains, and trenches, making the ocean floor as complex as geological formations found on land.

Haiti/Dominican Republic

Tobago

Trinidad

North coast of Venezuela

South America

Continental shelf

Guiana Plateau

Model (right) of a section of the sea floor east of the Caribbean, as shown in red square on map (below)

Continental slope

Arabian Sea

Pacific Ocean

Bering Sea

Sargasso Sea

Baltic Sea

Mediterranean Sea

Indian Ocean

Coral Sea

Tasman Sea

Southern Ocean

Caribbean Sea

Atlantic Ocean

OCEANS OF OCEANS
The world's five oceans, from the largest to the smallest, are the Pacific, the Atlantic, the Indian, the Southern, and the Arctic. The Pacific Ocean covers 166 million sq. km (64 million sq. miles) and is about 13 times the size of the Arctic Ocean. The Arctic Ocean's centre is permanently covered by a layer of sea ice which grows larger in winter and shrinks in summer when some of it melts. Over half the Southern Ocean is also frozen in winter, and sea ice still fringes the continent of Antarctica during the summer. The average depth of all the oceans in 3,650 m (12,000 ft) with the deepest part in the Pacific

GOD OF THE SEA
Neptune, the Roman god of the sea, seen here with a sea nymph, is usually depicted carrying a pronged trident, or spear and riding a dolphin. It was also thought he controlled freshwater supplies, so offerings were made to him during the driest months of the year.

FLOATING MEAL
The sea otter will float on its back in the calm of a kelp bed off the coasts of the Pacific Ocean rather than coming ashore. It feeds on sea-urchins and crustaceans floating in this position, crushing the hard shells with a stone.

FORMING A TRENCH
The gigantic plates on the earth's crust move like a conveyor belt. As new areas of ocean floor form, old areas disappear into the molten heart of the planet. This diagram shows one oceanic plate being forced under another to form the Mariana Trench. This process is called subduction, and here it creates an island arc.

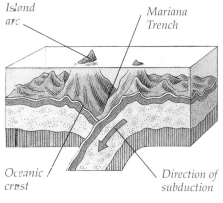

Island arc

Mariana Trench

Oceanic crust

Direction of subduction

Formation of Mariana Trench

Hatteras Abyssal Plain

Puerto Rico Trench

Nares Abyssal Plain

Mid-Atlantic Ridge

Kane Fracture Zone

Vema Fracture Zone

Demerara Abyssal Plain

OCEAN LANDSCAPE
This model shows the features on the bottom of the Atlantic Ocean off the northeast coast of South America from Guyana to Venezuela. Off this coast is the continental shelf, a region of relatively shallow water about 200 m (660 ft) deep. This continental shelf is about 200 km (125 miles) wide, but off the coast of northern Asia it is as much as 1,600 km (1,000 miles) wide. At the outer edge of the continental shelf, the ocean floor drops away steeply to form the continental slope. Sediments eroded from the land and carried by rivers such as the Orinoco accumulate at the bottom of the slope. The ocean floor then opens out in almost flat areas called abyssal plains, which are covered with a deep layer of soft sediments. The Puerto Rico Trench formed where one of the earth's plates, the North American Plate, is sliding past another, the Caribbean Plate. An arc of volcanic islands have also been created where the North American Plate is forced under the Caribbean Plate.

The coral kingdom

IN THE CRYSTAL-CLEAR, WARM WATERS of the tropics, coral reefs flourish, covering vast areas. The largest stony coral structure, Australia's Great Barrier Reef, alone stretches for 2,027 km (1,260 miles). Made of the skeletons of stony corals, coral reefs are cemented together by chalky algae. Most stony corals are colonies of many tiny, anemone-like individuals called polyps. Each polyp makes its own hard limestone cup (skeleton) which protects its soft body. To make their skeletons, the coral polyps need the help of microscopic, single-celled algae which live inside them. The algae need sunlight to grow, which is why coral reefs are found only in sunny, surface waters. In return for giving the algae a home, corals get some food from them but also capture plankton with their tentacles. Only the upper layer of a reef is made of living corals, which build upon skeletons of dead polyps. Coral reefs are also home to soft corals and sea fans, which do not have stony skeletons.

Tentacle's stings catch food

Mouth also expels waste

Hard plates of stony skeleton

Bag-like stomach

INSIDE A CORAL ANIMAL
In a stony coral, a layer of tissue joins each polyp to its neighbour. To reproduce, they divide in two or release eggs and sperm into the water.

Black coral's horny skeleton looks like a bunch of twigs

Orange sea fan
Eunicella verrucosa

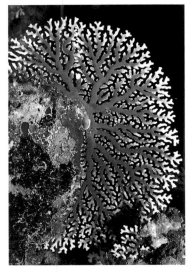

STINGING CORAL
Colourful hydrocorals are related to sea firs and, unlike horny and stony corals, produce jellyfish-like forms that carry their sex organs. Known as fire corals, they have potent stings on their polyps.

BLACK CORAL
In living black corals, the skeleton provides support for the living tissues and the branches bear rows of anemone-like polyps. Black corals are mainly found in tropical waters, growing in the deep part of coral reefs. Although they take a long time to grow, the black skeleton is sometimes used to make jewellery.

Intricate mesh developed to withstand strong currents

Stem of sea fan

162

SEA FAN
Sea fans are corals that have soft tissues growing around a central horny or chalky skeleton. They are more closely related to sea pens, organ-pipe coral, and soft corals than to true stony corals. Most kinds live in tropical waters where they often grow on coral reefs. Some sea fans form branching, tree-like shapes (left), but in others the branches join together to form a broad, fan-shaped network. From this structure the anemone-like polyps emerge to strain passing food from the water's currents.

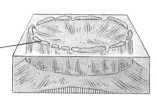

Fringing reef grows around volcano

As volcano subsides lagoon appears, creating barrier reef

Volcano disappears, leaving behind coral atoll

ATOLL IN THE MAKING
An atoll is a ring of coral islands formed around a central lagoon. Charles Darwin (1809–82) thought atolls were formed by a reef growing around a volcanic island which then subsided beneath the surface, a theory later proved to be correct.

Brittle skeleton of organ-pipe coral breaks easily

Branching tree-like skeleton

Queen scallops often make their home within the rose coral's folds

Living rose coral (not a true coral) can reach 50 cm (20 in) in diameter

Brain coral gets its name from its convoluted surface that looks like a human brain

ORGAN PIPES
Dull green-coloured tissue covers the bright red skeleton of living organ-pipe coral. Its anemone-like polyps emerge from each of the tiny pipes in the skeleton. Organ-pipe coral is not a true stony coral, but a relative of sea fans, soft coral, and sea pens.

A CORAL BY ANY OTHER NAME
Rose coral is a moss animal and grows in colonies on the seabed. Each colony is made of millions of tiny animals, each living in one unit in its leaf-like structure.

OLDEST CORALS
Australia's Great Barrier Reef has been formed gradually over a period of 600 million years and is the world's largest structure made by living organisms. Of the 350 kinds of coral found there, many spawn in their millions on the same night after a full moon, and resemble an underwater snowstorm.

STONE BRAIN
Living brain coral's surface is covered with soft tissue. Anemone-like polyps grow in rows along the channels in its skeleton. Brain corals are slow-growing stony corals, increasing in width a few centimetres each year.

Clown fish
*Amphiprion
percula*

Yellow
anemone

Clown anemone

Dangers of the reef

Coral reefs teem with life. Brightly-coloured fish and sea slugs swim in and out of the jagged landscape, shrimps hide in natural crevices in the coral, and sea horses cling to the seaweeds and sponges of the reef. Yet a coral reef is a dangerous place. Its changing surfaces provide both shelter and opportunity for prey and predator alike. Most of the hunted sea creatures, like small wrasse, must feed out in the open. However, at a second's notice, they can dart out of harm's way by digging themselves into loose sand or mud, or diving into a narrow cleft in the rocks. Hunters like the mandarin fish and the common octopus (pp. 78–79) are content to lurk inside coral caves, watching for unsuspecting victims to move close enough. And there are other dangers – many sea creatures have to avoid the deadly embrace of poisonous sea anemones and meat-eating corals. Sometimes, however, a dangerous situation can be turned to advantage. The clown fish lays its eggs and even rears its young safely among the tentacles of the clown anemone, which catches and eats other small fish.

CLOWNING AROUND
On many tropical reefs, gaily-coloured clown fish dart among the tentacles of a sea anemone that carries a venomous sting which would paralyze other small fish in seconds. Clown fish have an especially thick body covering that does not contain the usual substances which stimulate the anemone to sting. The anemone absorbs pieces of food dropped by its colourful visitors.

Eyespots give impression of huge "face"

Loose gravel for wrasse to dive into

1 SELF-PROTECTION
The twinspot wrasse has two large eyespots on its dorsal fin. If this huge "face" fails to frighten predators, the twinspot uses alternative means to avoid danger. A threatening sound, worrying scent, or an actual sighting of a predator makes the twinspot tilt its head down. As it dives, it searches out a bare patch of shell fragments and gravel for refuge.

2 TESTING THE BED
As the twinspot reaches the seabed, it swerves up to a horizontal position and thrusts its sensitive snout and chest into the gravel. Sometimes this turns out to be only a shallow layer on top of solid rock and no use for hiding.

Ray of dorsal fin

Mandarin fish
*Synchiropus
splendidus*

Seahorse
*Hippocampus
kuda*

*Seahorse's eyes
move independently*

*Long, hollow
snout to suck
up shrimps*

NASTY TASTE
The brilliant colours of its skin warn other sea
creatures that the mandarin fish tastes nasty. It
produces a slimy mucus in the skin that smells and tastes
unpleasant. The mucus helps to protect the fish from attack by
bacteria and fungi, as well as larger fish. The mandarin fish lives
near the seabed and feeds on smaller fish and other creatures
that float past. It also nibbles at the algae on the coral reef.

CHANGING COLOUR
Seahorses cannot swim fast to escape danger, but they
can change colour to match their background and hide
from enemies. They anchor themselves with their
strong, supple tail to coral or seaweeds and wait for
food, such as prawns, to swim past. To
rise up, the seahorse straightens its tail,
curling it to sink. The fin on its back
bends backwards and forwards to push
the seahorse through the water.

*Loose gravel
flung upwards
by wrasse's
activity*

3 DIGGING IN
Throwing its body into S-shaped curves, and
digging down in a diagonal direction, the twinspot
"swims" head first into the loose gravel and stones. Its
fins and tail fling the gravel upwards out of the way.
Within seconds, the fish is settled into the surface layer
of stones, and the falling gravel rains back down to
add to its covering. The twinspot stays without
moving until it senses that things are back to normal
above. Many species of wrasse, especially round the
Pacific coral islands, bury themselves in the gravel
each night and go to "sleep" there.

Strawberry
shrimp
*Lysmata
debelius*

SHY SHRIMP
The strawberry shrimp hides
in natural crevices in coral or
digs a burrow in the sand with its
chelipeds (claws). The shrimp grows
in spurts, increasing in size each
time it moults. It has to hide
away from enemies, such as
fish and crabs, while the
soft new exoskeleton
stretches and hardens.

*Complete layer of
gravel hides wrasse
from predators*

Tropical storms

Hurricane force winds often damage buildings

KNOWN AS TYPHOONS IN THE PACIFIC, and tropical cyclones by meteorologists, hurricanes claim more lives each year than any other storm. When a full-blown hurricane strikes, trees are uprooted and buildings flattened by raging winds that gust at up to 360 km/h (220 mph). Vast areas are swamped by torrential rain, and coastal regions can be overwhelmed by the "storm surge".

This is a wall of water some 8 m (26 ft) high, sucked up by the storm's "eye" – the ring of low pressure at the storm's centre – and topped by giant waves whipped up by the winds. Hurricanes begin as small thunderstorms over warm, tropical oceans. If the water is warm enough (over 24°C or 75°F), several storms may whirl around as one, encouraged by strong winds high in the atmosphere. Soon they drift westward across the ocean, drawing in warm, moist air and spinning in tighter circles. At first, the centre of the storm may be over 330 km (200 miles) across, and the winds just gale force. As it moves west, it gains energy from the warm air it sucks in. By the time the storm reaches the far side of the ocean, the eye has shrunk to 50 km (30 miles) across, pressure has dropped, and winds howl around it at hurricane force.

ANATOMY OF A HURRICANE
The air in the eye of the hurricane is at low pressure. As the eye passes over, the winds may drop altogether, and a small circle of clear sky become visible for a while. The lull is short-lived as torrential rains fall around the eye, and raging winds, drawn in from hot air that spirals up its wall, circulate at speeds of 50 km/h (30 mph). Spiralling bands of rain and wind can occur up to 400 km (240 miles) away. It can be 18 hours or more before the storm has passed over.

MIXED BLESSING
The vegetation and agriculture on many tropical islands depend on the torrential rains brought by hurricanes. But the terrible winds can also ravage crops, and only a few – like bananas – recover quickly.

The strongest winds, with gusts up to 360 km/h (220 mph), are found beneath the eye wall, immediately outside the eye

HURRICANE WATCH
Thanks to satellite images, meteorologists can detect hurricanes when they are far from land, and track them as they approach. Special aircraft repeatedly fly through the storm to obtain accurate measurements that help predict its violence and likely path. Since 1954, names have been given to all tropical storms to prevent confusion when issuing forecasts and evacuation warnings.

 1 Day 1: Thunderstorms develop over the sea.

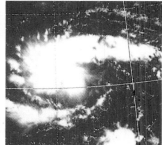 2 Day 2: Storms group to form a swirl of cloud.

 3 Day 4: Winds grow; centre forms in cloud swirl.

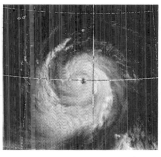 4 Day 7: Eye forms; typhoon is at its most dangerous.

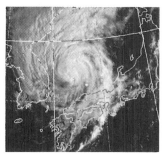 5 Day 11: Eye passes over land; typhoon starts to die.

PACIFIC HURRICANE

The sequence above shows satellite images of a typhoon passing over the Pacific Ocean. It begins when water evaporates in the tropical sun over vast areas of the ocean to produce huge cumulonimbus clouds and bands of thunderstorms (1). A swirl of clouds develops, and the growing storm looks like a vigorous, ordinary depression (2). The winds become even stronger, and rotate around a single centre (3). Eventually, an eye develops, just inside the ring of the most destructive and violent winds (4). When such a storm passes over land – in this case, Japan – or over cold seas, it loses its source of energy, and the winds drop rapidly (5).

Warm, moist air spirals up around the eye inside the hurricane

Hurricanes are enormous; some may be as much as 800 km (480 miles) across

The heat contained by the warm sea provides the energy needed to drive the whole system

Air descends in the eye, leaving it clear of cloud

ALBANY HURRICANE

Hurricanes were far more dangerous before the strength of their approach could be predicted. In 1940, the fringes of a hurricane struck Albany, Georgia, USA, without adequate warning, killing several people, and wrecking large numbers of buildings, including big hotels. Two years before, 600 people were killed in New England by a sudden, fast-moving storm.

Winds of more than 165 km/h (100 mph) occur over a large area beneath the storm

Ocean giants

THE BIGGEST WHALE – and the biggest animal that has ever lived – is the blue whale. Only other baleen whales and the sperm whale come anywhere near its enormous size. The largest living land animal, the bull elephant, could stand on a blue whale's tongue! Even the biggest dinosaur weighed less than a quarter of a large blue whale. Such size has its benefits. Big animals are less likely to be attacked by predators, and it is easier for them to keep warm. Their main problem is to find enough food to nourish their awesome bulk.

Pectoral fin

WHALE LICE
A number of animals make their homes on the great expanse of a whale's skin. Some are harmless hangers-ons, but others, like this whale louse, probably irritate the skin.

Tail flukes

TALL TAIL
Unlike some baleen whales, blue whales raise their tails in the air when they dive.

Stubby dorsal fin

A WHALE OF AN APPETITE
It is no coincidence that whale sharks, the world's largest fish, are also filter feeders. Because animals that feed on plankton do not need to chase individual prey, they do not have to be agile. This has allowed some to grow to great sizes. Whale sharks do not have baleen plates. Instead, they filter food from the water with their gills.

THE WORLD'S BIGGEST BABY
The day it is born, a baby blue whale is already as big as an elephant. It has no baleen plates, and relies entirely on its giant mother's milk. Like seal milk, this is very high in fat. Every day the growing whale drinks about 100 litres (175 pints) of milk and puts on another 90 kg (200 lb). By the time it is weaned, after the age of six or seven months, the young blue whale is already 16 m (52 ft) long.

Baby blue whales often breach when only a few weeks old

Adult blue whales can weigh 200 tonnes

WHALE OUT OF WATER
Whales can only reach such incredible sizes because their weight is supported by the water. When a large whale like this sperm whale is stranded, it cannot support its own weight and its internal organs are crushed.

BLUE SPLASH
No one knows why whales breach – leap out of the water. Adults often breach in the company of other whales, and this suggests that the big splash is a way of communicating. Young animals like this baby blue may start breaching when they are only a few weeks old. Perhaps by playing they are learning skills which will be important to them as adults.

Paired blow-holes

THE BIG BLUE
Blue whales grow to more than 32 m (104 ft) and can weigh up to 200 tonnes. They were hunted mercilessly in the southern oceans, and most of the information about them comes from the whaling industry. Weights were estimated by measuring chopped-off chunks and adding a few tonnes to make up for lost blood. Even the lengths may be incorrect, as the whales could have been stretched by towing. Blue whales received complete protection from whalers in 1966. But there are no signs that numbers have increased, and there may be only a few hundred left in the entire southern oceans.

Throat grooves allow baleen whales to gulp down huge amounts of water

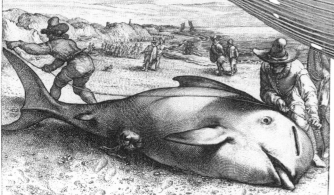

PILOT STUDY
Measuring a stranded whale is easy. But how do you measure a live whale at sea? One way is to take a series of photos as the whale surfaces. By lining them end to end, scientists can piece together the animal's entire length.

Vents and smokers

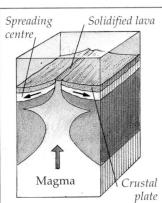

Spreading centre   *Solidified lava*

Magma   *Crustal plate*

A CHANGING OCEAN
New areas of ocean floor are continually being created at spreading centres between two crustal plates. When hot, molten lava (melted rock) emerges from the crust, it cools and solidifies along the edge of each adjoining plate.

IN PARTS OF THE OCEAN FLOOR, there are cracks. From these gush very hot, mineral-rich water. These dramatic vents or hot springs exist at the spreading centres where the gigantic plates that make up the earth's crust are moving apart. Cold seawater sinks deep into cracks in the crust. There, the water is heated, in the process collecting dissolved minerals. At temperatures of up to 400°C (752°F), hot water spews out, and some of the minerals form chimneys that are known as black or white smokers. Hot water produced by the vents helps bacteria grow, and they create food from the hydrogen sulphide in the water. Extraordinary animals crowd around the cracks and rely on these microbes for food. The vents are independent of energy from the sun, relying instead on a chemical reaction from bacteria in the sulphur. As recently as the late 1970s, scientists using submersibles found the first vent communities in the Pacific. Since then, vents have been found in spreading centres in the Pacific Ocean and the Mid-Atlantic Ridge.

SEEPING LAVA
Under the huge pressure of the ocean water, the lava from vents or hot springs erupts constantly and gently, like toothpaste squeezed from a tube, and cools to form rounded shapes known as pillow lava (above). Where there is a spreading ridge, the water is hot, acidic, and black with sulphides of copper, lead, and zinc. These valuable metals come from the new oceanic plate that is formed at the ridges. The minerals are dissolved out by seawater that percolates through the cooling rock.

DEEP SEA PRAWNS
Animal life abounds in an active vent site. If the vent stops producing sulphur-rich water, the community is doomed. This new species of prawn was found at the Galápagos Rift in the Pacific Ocean in 1979.

Fish predators nibble tops off tube worms

Model of hydrothermal vents found in the eastern Pacific

VENT COMMUNITIES
This model shows the vent communities that have been found in the eastern Pacific, where giant clams and tube worms are the most distinctive animals. Vents in other parts of the world have different groups of animals, such as the hairy snails from the Mariana Trench, and the eyeless shrimps found near vents along the Mid-Atlantic Ridge.

Giant clams in the eastern Pacific can grow to 30 cm (12 in) long

Some animals graze on mats of bacteria covering rocks near a vent

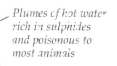

Plumes of hot water rich in sulphides and poisonous to most animals

Black smoker chimney can reach 10 m (33 ft)

Chimney made from mineral deposits

Dense numbers of animals crowd round a vent

THE MID-ATLANTIC RIDGE

The rocks that make up the ocean floor are all young – nowhere older than 200 million years. This is because new ocean plates are constantly being made by volcanic eruptions deep below the ocean waters. A long range of mountains snakes through the oceans, cut at its heart by a rift valley. The volcanoes in this rift valley erupt constantly, producing new volcanic rock. The new rock fills in the widening rift as the plates pull apart. The Mid-Atlantic Ridge (above), running the length of the Atlantic Ocean between Europe and Africa on the east and the Americas on the west, is part of the largest mountain range in the world.

Tube worms, Riftia pachyptila, can grow to 3 m (10 ft) long

Giant tube worm has bacteria inside its body, to provide the worm with food

The darkest depths

THERE IS NO NATURAL LIGHT in the oceans
below 1,000 m (3,000 ft), just inky blackness.
Many fish there are black too, making them
almost invisible. However, they use light
organs as signals to find a mate or to lure
prey. Food is scarce and all the animals
have to rely on what little floats down from
above. Deep-sea fish make the most of this
food by having huge mouths and stretchy
stomachs. Often the fish are small or weigh
very little because of their lightweight
bones and muscles. This means they can
maintain neutral buoyancy – they can keep
at one level without having to swim.

*Lateral line
organs sense
vibrations in water
made by moving prey*

UMBRELLA MOUTH GULPER
With its large mouth open wide, the gulper
eel swims along, swallowing any food, such
as shrimps and small fish, that it comes across.
The young stages resemble the leaf-like larvae
of European eels and are found in the sunlit zone,
100–200 m (330–660 ft), where food is plentiful.
As they grow, young gulper eels descend into
deeper waters. Adult gulper eels live in the
lower part of the twilight zone at 200–1,000 m
(660–3,300 ft) as well as in the dark zone,
1,000–4,000 m (3,300–13,200 ft).

*Adult gulper eel,
Eupharynx pelecanoides*

Tiny eye on end of nose

*Adults grow to
about 75 cm (30 in)
from head to the tip
of their long tails*

*Adults live in dark
depths below temperate
and tropical surface waters*

*Long lower jaw scoops
up food from the water*

FISHING LINE
The whipnose lives in the Atlantic and Pacific
Oceans. It uses its lure to draw prey closer to
its mouth. Unlike a true fishing line, the
whipnose's nose does not have a
hook on the end. The lure
may also be used to
help a male fish
recognize females
of their own
species.

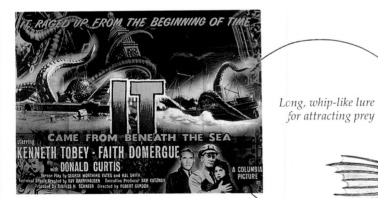

MONSTER MOVIES
Films about scary monsters are always popular,
and especially those from the pitch-black ocean
depths. So little of the deep ocean has been
explored that there could be strange animals yet
to be discovered. But most deep-sea animals are
small, as there is so little food at these depths.

*Long, whip-like lure
for attracting prey*

*Whipnose grows to 13 cm
(5 in) in length*

*Model of a whipnose
Gigantactis macronema*

BINOCULAR EYES
Gigantura's extraordinary tubular eyes
are probably used to pinpoint the glowing
light organs of its prey. Even though *Gigantura* has
a narrow body, its skin can stretch so that it is able
to swallow fish larger than itself.

*Lower lobe of tail
fin longer than
upper lobe*

GOING FISHING
Angler fish are not just found in the ocean depths. This one, from shallow waters, uses a worm-like lure on the end of its dorsal fin ray as a lure. A fish swimming by, tempted to bite the worm, will end up inside the angler's stomach.

Model of angler fish before a meal

Lure contains luminous bacteria used to attract prey and males

Dorsal fin ray

Small eye typical of fish of the dark zone

Teeth bend backwards to allow passage of large prey into mouth

Caudal fin

Model of angler fish, *Melanocetus johnsoni*, after a meal

Big, stretchy stomach allows deep-sea angler fish to take huge meals

ANGLERS
One angler fish was found with a lantern fish twice its own size in its stomach. The prey is attracted to the gaping jaws by a glow-in-the-dark lure on the end of a long fin ray. Large teeth, curving backward, make sure that the angler does not let go of its prey once it is within reach. The prey is not chewed up, but swallowed whole.

Extraordinary eyes look like binoculars

TOUGH JELLY
Found in all the world's oceans, *Atolla* jellyfish are as tough as fruit gums. They are typically reddish-brown and, like all other jellyfish, have stinging tentacles to catch prey. If disturbed, *Atolla* glows in the dark, sending out a bluish light that lasts for several seconds.

Model of *Gigantura*

Ocean wanderers

THE HUGE, GENTLE ALBATROSSES of the Antarctic seas come ashore only to breed. They do not breed on the Antarctic land mass itself but on islands such as South Georgia, just north of the pack ice. There are six species of albatross breeding in the Antarctic: the black-browed, grey-headed, wandering, yellow-nosed, sooty, and light-mantled sooty. Probably about 750,000 pairs of birds breed each year, the main advantage of these isolated locations being safety from predators. Albatrosses raise only one chick at a time and the chick takes a long time to mature, sometimes remaining in the nest for up to a year. Chicks are protected from the intense cold by thick down feathers and an insulating layer of fat or blubber. When winter sets in, most albatrosses set off over the southern oceans once more.

A man weighed down by more than grief: albatrosses can weigh up to 12 kg (25 lb)

DEAD WEIGHT
Sailors believed albatrosses brought them good luck. In Coleridge's *The Rime of the Ancient Mariner,* the unlucky mariner is forced to wear an albatross he has killed.

Wings very long and slender for effortless gliding above the ocean

Black-browed albatross
Diomedea melanophris

BUMPY LANDING
Landing is a difficult task for a bird so well adapted to flying over the sea. When albatrosses approach the nest site, they circle round several times, before putting their legs down, like the landing gear on an aircraft. But they often land with a bump.

Webbed feet held wide to push against the air and act as brakes

Grey-headed albatross
Diomedea chrysostoma

Large eyes indicate sharp eyesight needed for spotting food in the sea

BIRD MAN
People have always wanted to fly like birds but this design for an early flying machine was no challenge to the albatross's mastery of the air. For birds, as with planes, take-off and landing are the most dangerous parts of flying. Like planes, albatrosses need a runway to gather enough speed for take-off. Without this, their enormous wingspan and body weight make sure that they remain firmly earthbound.

Tube-shaped nostrils have glands at the base that excrete excess salt

Bill has razor-sharp edges to catch fish and squid

LIVING THE HIGH LIFE
Grey-headed albatrosses live on steep cliff sides because they need the strong winds rising up over the cliffs to help them take off. Although grey-headed albatrosses weigh half as much as wandering albatrosses, only half of their chicks survive because the parent birds cannot find and bring back enough food to keep the young alive.

During courtship the bird points its beak to the sky and moos like a cow

FAITHFUL FLYING ACE

The wandering albatross has the greatest wingspan of any living bird. Its wing power enables the bird to cover as much as 500 km (300 miles) a day, alighting on the sea in calm weather or to feed. Like all albatrosses, it comes ashore only to breed. The breeding cycle is exceptionally long, taking a year to complete. It therefore breeds only every two years. The bird precedes breeding by an elaborate courtship display, in which the two birds dance face to face making a variety of weird sounds, and clapping their beaks together loudly Wandering albatrosses usually pair for life. The most elaborate displays take place among newly formed pairs; old established partners are more discreet.

Wingspan may be 254–360 cm (8 ft 4 in– 11 ft 10 in)

SECONDHAND FOOD

Parent albatrosses feed their young by regurgitating (bringing up) the seafood they eat in the form of a sticky, oily mixture. This takes place when they return to the nest after many hours, or even days, fishing out at sea. Both adults and young can use this smelly and sticky oil in defence, ejecting it with reasonable accuracy over a couple of metres (6 ft) range. Predators, such as skuas, may be repelled by the foul smell or immobilized if the sticky oil saturates their feathers.

Mother feeds regurgitated krill to chick

Nest is lined with grass and feathers

Nest is about 30 cm (12 in) high

BARREL NEST
The black-browed albatross makes a raised nest of mud and straw among the tussock grass.

Wandering albatross
Diomedea irrorata

Strong legs and wide feet assist landing and swimming

GENTLE GIANT
The largest of all the land mammals, the elephant has the longest of all pregnancies – 22 months – and one calf is born at a time. Like many other large mammals, elephants spend considerable energy and time in nurturing their young, a strategy that helps ensure that the calf survives to breed. Unfortunately, the continued existence of the African elephant is threatened because, except in wildlife reserves, elephants and people are often competing for the same territory.

VULNERABLE PLANTS

There are many species of plant under threat, including the shade-loving aroid *Alocasia thibautiana* that can grow in the gloomiest parts of the jungles of southeast Asia. The fern *Diplazium proliferum* thrives best on the jungle floor where it is warm and damp. This fern produces bulbils on its fronds which will sprout and take root, either when they are knocked off the plant, or the frond dies.

Alocasia thibautiana

WALLS OF DEATH

Drift nets are like invisible curtains. In the open ocean, big fishing boats use drift nets up to 50 km (30 miles) long. If the nets get tangled, the fishermen often just cut them and let them drift off. Huge numbers of whales, dolphins, and seals are killed when they swim into these free-floating traps. The United Nations has banned long drift nets, but some countries are not members of the UN, and the laws are impossible to enforce in the open ocean.

Dense, waterproof coat turns grey-white in winter

Velvet contains blood vessels to nourish the growing antlers

Reindeer or caribou *Rangifer tarandus*

Sensitive nose helps reindeer find food even under snow

IN THE SNOW

Many animals and plants live in difficult habitats, where food or water are hard to find. Reindeer feed mainly on lichens, which are one of the few foods available throughout the Arctic winter. Some reindeer living on Arctic islands will also eat seaweed. Calves are born in June and grow fast on their mother's rich milk, which is four times as nutritious as cow's milk. Although their thick coats insulate the reindeer from the Arctic cold, they migrate south in the winter to find food and shelter.

Sharp hooves grip ice and dig through snow for food

179

Studying populations

THE WAYS IN WHICH both animal and plant
populations grow and decrease tell scientists
a lot about species and their ability to survive.
Lemmings provide a vivid example of this.
These small rodents inhabit the cold northern
regions of the northern hemisphere.
Every three to four years, the lemming
population grows so much that they
migrate in large numbers – something
that scientists think is caused by the
animals outstripping food supplies.
Tales of lemmings committing suicide
are based on the fact that they swim across
rivers in search of food. On migration,
when they reach the sea, they attempt
to cross that as well, and drown as a result.
This natural cull reduces lemming numbers
to an appropriate size for their food supply.

White feathers for
winter camouflage

Snowy owl
Nyctea scandiaca

PREDATOR AND PREY
The snowy owl, seen here swooping down on a vole, lives mainly
in the tundra of North America and Eurasia where it is normally
a rare sight. However, every three or four years, snowy owls
suddenly appear in large numbers, and invade towns across
the United States, even as far south as Georgia. This strange
phenomenon appears to be linked to the population changes of
the lemming, on which the snowy owl feeds. As the lemmings
reach plague proportions, the snowy owls, provided with a
plentiful food supply, increase rapidly in numbers. When
the lemmings migrate, the owls too migrate in search
of food, dispersing over a wide area, their numbers
dropping to low levels for the next two years as
the number of lemmings available drops.

Powerful claw with long
talons for gripping

Owl looks for
movement of prey
before swooping

MIGRATION PATTERNS
Voles in northern latitudes (left) have a similar population
cycle to the lemming, perhaps based on the cycle of plant
growth. As the size of the population increases, more and
more of the vital nutrients in the environment become
locked up in the form of droppings. In the cold
conditions of the Arctic, where
decomposition takes a long
time, these nutrients are
released very slowly. Plant
growth suffers, causing
the rodents to leave the
area to look for food. The
vegetation can only begin
to recover when the voles
or lemmings migrate.

Large, powerful wing

MARKING

By marking an animal, its habits and movements can be traced, but the marking must be done carefully to avoid influencing the animal's behaviour. This bird is having a ring fitted to its leg. Fish sometimes have a tag attached to the fin, and some mammals are tagged through the ear. A larger animal may be fitted with a radio collar, and its movements tracked with a radio receiver.

Growth rings on magnified fish scale

SIGNS OF GROWING

An animal's age can be worked out in several ways, such as looking at the wear on a mammal's teeth. In the case of fish, the scales provide a useful indication of age, revealing dark rings that are formed each year during the winter, when the growth is at its slowest. Ecologists use this information to determine the age structure of a fish population, calculate how it will change over a period of time, and decide how many fish can be caught without putting the population at risk.

Sampling populations

An understanding of how populations of fish, pests, crops, or rare animals behave has practical benefits for food production and for conservation. Population studies provide information about the number of individuals in a population and the number found in a given area (the population density), the changes in population over time, the birth rate, and the death rate. Since it is impossible to collect an entire population, this information must be gained by capturing a few members and estimating the figures from this sample. Such samples are the basis for much of our scientific understanding of populations.

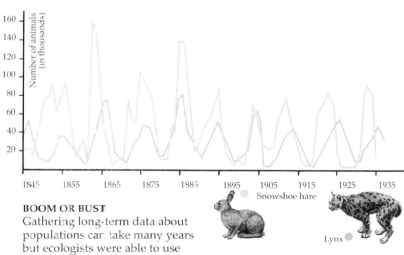

Snowshoe hare

Lynx

TRAPS AND TRAPPING

Nets are used to catch birds and fish for study, but mammals such as this Australian bandicoot must be attracted to elaborate traps if they are to be released unharmed. The animal's favourite food is usually placed in the trap as bait.

BOOM OR BUST

Gathering long-term data about populations can take many years but ecologists were able to use historical records from the Hudson's Bay Company to produce this population graph of two species in the Canadian Arctic. It shows that every nine or ten years the number of snowshoe hares rises to a peak and then drops dramatically. The lynx population follows closely behind that of the snowshoe hare, on which the lynx depends for food. This "boom or bust" cycle, which is still not fully understood, is characteristic of several animal species living in extreme environmental conditions.

Surviving

NATURE IS A finely-tuned balancing act and no one living thing can survive without some dependence on, or ability to affect, another. All animals and plants need energy and materials from the environment, and they survive despite the precarious nature of food chains, living in difficult environments, and having to cope with the additional problems of bad weather, disease, and pollution. The adaptability of life on earth is endlessly ingenious. For example, in cold places where there are few insects to pollinate, many plants reproduce from small pieces of themselves such as runners or bulbils. Some animals, such as the polar bear and the fox, have even benefited from the creation of towns and cities, changing their diet and scavenging on human refuse.

SPECIAL ADAPTATIONS
A camel is well suited to desert conditions because it can go for weeks without water. It conserves moisture because its body temperature can rise many degrees before the animal starts to sweat. It also uses the fat stores in its hump. The fat is gradually used up if it does not eat enough, and as the fat is depleted, the hump shrinks.

Northern fleabane
Erigeron borealis

LIVING FOSSIL
Some species survive for millions of years. The coelacanth is a fish that was thought to be extinct; all the known fossils were more than 200 million years old. Then, in 1938, a live coelacanth was fished out of the ocean. If such a creature can survive for 200 million years without leaving any fossils, it is not surprising that some steps in the evolution of life on earth are not recorded.

Colouring very similar to coral snake

MISLEADING COLOURS
Many creatures have evolved ways of protecting themselves from predators. This harmless Sinaloan milk snake looks very like the highly venomous coral snake. This happy chance may deter quite a few predators from trying to make a meal of the snake. Milk snakes are so-called because of a mistaken belief that they steal milk from cows.

Sinaloan milk snake
Lampropeltis doliata

HARDY PLANTS
In order to survive, many plants have evolved in special ways. Low cushions of northern fleabane flower in the Arctic summer when the tundra lands become waterlogged. The plant grows in a low, compact tussock to keep out of the freezing, drying wind, to trap available moisture, and to avoid being crushed by snow and ice.

Krill are omnivores, eating phytoplankton, other crustaceans, and other krill

Krill sieve food from water with their feathery feeding apparatus

At night, the luminescent organs of krill shimmer in the darkness

Bulbous eyes

Female krill spawn twice a year, laying 2,000–3,000 eggs, which sink into deep water

Krill are just 5 cm (2 in) long, but sometimes occur in such vast numbers that the sea appears to be coloured red

CAREFUL PARENTING
Survival of a species is dependent on the species' ability to produce young. This female leaf beetle guarding her young family produces relatively few of them, but by protecting them in early life, she increases their chances of survival. Some animals produce very few young and invest considerable time and energy in raising them. Others produce huge numbers of offspring, but do nothing to look after them. A female cod, for example, lays over a million eggs, but nearly all are eaten before they have a chance to grow into adults.

FOOD SOURCES
The shrimp-like crustacean krill is the basis of most of the Antarctic food chains, forming a vital food source for whales and seals, as well as penguins and other seabirds. A blue whale needs more than 900 kg (1,980 lb) of krill to feel full and eats about four tonnes of krill a day! The reduction in whale numbers caused by human hunting in the past have made krill numbers increase. Other krill-eating species such as penguins and fur seals increased in number to exploit the extra food source, upsetting the balance of existing food webs. The long-term repercussions of this kind of change are as yet unknown.

Glossary

ALGAE Simple plants that do not have true stems, roots, or leaves, but contain chlorophyll. Most are found in water.
See also CHLOROPHYLL.

AMOEBA A tiny, simple animal that has no fixed shape and lives in water.

AMPHIBIAN Cold-blooded and smooth-skinned vertebrate that begins life in the water, but can live on land when it is adult; for example, a frog, toad, or salamander.
See also VERTEBRATE.

ANTENNA One of a pair of flexible feelers on the head of some animals, such as insects or crustaceans.
See also CRUSTACEAN.

ANTHER The upper part of the stamen of a flowering plant.
See also STAMEN.

ARTHROPOD Creature with segmented covering and jointed limbs. Includes insects, crustaceans, arachnids, and centipedes.
See also CRUSTACEAN.

BACTERIUM (pl. bacteria) Microorganism that brings about decomposition; or a parasite, many of which cause disease.

BAROMETER Instrument for measuring atmospheric pressure used in weather forecasting.

BIOSPHERE Regions of the earth and its atmosphere in which living things are found.

BIVALVE A mollusc with a shell consisting of two hinged parts. Includes oysters, cockles, clams, scallops, and mussels.
See also MOLLUSC.

BYSSAL THREADS Mass of threads that bivalves use to attach themselves to rocks.
See also BIVALVE.

CAECILIAN Legless, burrowing amphibian found in tropical regions.
See also AMPHIBIAN.

CAMOUFLAGE Colour, markings, or shape of an animal or plant that enable it to hide in its surroundings.

CARNIVOROUS Meat-eating.

CARPEL The central, female part of a flower, consisting of an ovary, style, and stigma.

CELL The smallest unit of an organism that can exist on its own.

CEPHALOPOD Mollusc with a beaked head and tentacles. Includes the octopus and nautilus.
See also MOLLUSC.

CHELONIAN Belonging to the Chelonia, a group of reptiles that includes turtles.

CHLOROPHYLL Green pigment found in plants that traps energy from sunlight.
See also PIGMENT.

CHLOROPLAST Tiny body in some plant cells that contains chlorophyll.
See also CHLOROPHYLL.

CHRYSALIS The stage of life between caterpillar and the adult butterfly or moth.

CILIA Hairlike growths from the surface of a cell or organism.
See also CELL.

COCOON Covering of silk spun by the larvae of moths and other insects to protect them in their pupa stage.
See also LARVA.

COELENTERATE Invertebrate animal with sacklike internal cavity. Includes jellyfish, sea anemones, and cords.

COMPOUND EYE Eye of most insects made up of separate lenses that work as individual eyes, each forming a part of the image.

CROSS-POLLINATION The transfer of pollen from the stamens of one plant to the stigma of another.
See also STAMEN.

CRUSTACEAN Usually aquatic group of animals with a segmented body and paired, jointed limbs. Includes lobsters, crabs, shrimps, and wood lice.

DECOMPOSER Something that breaks down dead organic matter, such as a bacterium or fungus.
See also BACTERIUM, FUNGUS.

DIAPAUSE A period during which certain insects do not grow or develop.

DIATOM Minute, single-celled algae.
See also ALGAE.

ECHO-LOCATION A way of finding objects by sending out sounds, then listening for the echo. Bats use echo-location to navigate.

ECOSYSTEM A complete area in the biosphere which contains living things, such as a forest.

ELEMENT A substance that cannot be broken down into more simple substances by chemical reactions.

ENDOSPERM The tissue that surrounds and feeds the embryo of a flowering plant.

ENVIRONMENT The surroundings of plants or animals – the environment affects the way they live.

EPIDERMIS The outer layer of the skin.

EVAPORATION The changing of a liquid into a vapour by the escape of molecules from its surface.

EXOSKELETON The hard, outer skin of arthropods.
See also ARTHROPOD.

FOSSIL The ancient remains of a plant or animal, usually found in rocks. A fossil may be the actual bones of an animal or the shape left by the animal's body in the rock.

FOSSIL FUEL Flammable material that comes from the remains of animals and plants that lived millions of years ago. Includes coal and oil.

FUNGUS One of a group of organisms that lack chlorophyll and are usually parasitic.
See also CHLOROPHYLL.

GASTROPOD A mollusc with a coiled shell and a large, muscular foot that it uses to move.
See also MOLLUSC.

GERMINATION In plants, when seeds or spores sprout.

GILLS Parts of fish that is used for breathing underwater.

HABITAT A place where an animal or plant usually lives; woodlands, grasslands, and mountains are examples of different habitats.

HERBIVOROUS Plant-eating.

HIBERNATE To sleep deeply or remain still through the winter in order to conserve energy and survive the winter.

INCUBATION The warming of eggs by bodily heat or other means to encourage the growth and hatching of young.

INVERTEBRATE An animal with no backbone.

LARVA The second stage in the life of an insect that occurs between the egg and the emergence of the adult. Tadpoles and caterpillars are larvae.

LAVA Hot, liquid rock that flows from deep inside the earth. The lava cools and hardens when it reaches the surface.

MAGMA Melted rock beneath the earth's crust.

MAMMAL Warm-blooded animal that gives birth to live young that feed on the mother's milk.

MANDIBLE Jaw or sharp, hard part of an insect's mouthparts. Most insects have two mandibles.

MANTLE The layer of the earth that lies beneath the surface and the centre.

MARSUPIAL A mammal which has a pouch on the outside of its body in which its young develop.

METAMORPHOSIS The transformation of an animal during growth. Includes the emergence of an adult fly from a maggot, a butterfly from a caterpillar, and a frog from a tadpole.

METEOROLOGIST Scientist who studies weather and weather conditions.

MICROBE Tiny, living organism that can only be seen with a microscope.
See also ORGANISM.

MIGRATION Moving from one place to another. Animals migrate to find food, produce young, or escape from cold weather.

MOLLUSC An animal with a soft body that usually lives in a shell. Snails, limpets, and slugs are molluscs.

MONOTREME One of a group of egg-laying animals that lives in Australia and New Guinea. Includes the platypus and the echidna.

MUTUALISM Relationship between two or more animals, in which all benefit.

NECTARIES Glandlike organ at the base of a flower in which nectar is stored.

NEMATOCYST Stinging organ in coelenterates such as jellyfish.
See also COELENTERATE.

NUCLEUS The centre of an atom, a nucleus is made up of electrically charged protons and of neutrons.

NYMPH A young insect, a nymph looks like its parents, but does not have any wings.

OCELLUS (pl. ocelli) A small, simple eye found in many vertebrates.
See also VERTEBRATE.

ORGANISM Any living plant or animal.

PALAEONTOLOGIST Scientist who studies fossils and ancient life forms.
See also FOSSIL.

PARASITE An organism that grows and feeds on or in another organism, but does not contribute to the survival of the host
See also ORGANISM.

PHOTOSYNTHESIS The way that plants make food by using energy from sunlight and turning carbon dioxide and water into sugars

PHYTOPLANKTON Minute, floating aquatic plants.

PIGMENT A substance, such as chlorophyll, that produces a particular colour in plant or animal tissue.
See also CHLOROPHYLL.

PLACENTAL Having a placenta, the organ that develops in female mammals during pregnancy to provide the foetus with the nutrients that it needs.

PNEUMATOPHORE A gas-filled sac that serves as a float for colonies such as the jellyfish Portuguese man-of-war.

POLLINATOR The animal that carries pollen from one flower to another to help make seeds. Insects are the most common pollinators.

POLYP A coelenterate with a cylindrical body and tentacles, such as coral.

PREDATOR An animal that lives by hunting and eating other animals.

PREY An animal that is hunted and eaten by another animal.

PRIMATE A member of the mammal group that includes gorillas, monkeys, chimpanzees, and human beings.
See also MAMMAL

PROBOSCIS A tube for feeding and sucking in some insects.

PROMINENCE A bright spout of gas reaching out from the sun's surface into space.

PUPA The last stage in the life of some young insects. The pupa is the resting stage during which the adult takes shape.

RADICLE The part of the plant that develops into the primary root.

REPTILE One of a group of animals with dry, scaly skin that usually lay eggs with shells. Includes snakes, turtles, and crocodiles.

RESPIRATION The process of inhaling and exhaling; the process by which an organism takes in oxygen, releasing carbon dioxide and energy.
See also ORGANISM.

RODENT An animal with long, front teeth which are used for gnawing. Includes mice, rats, and squirrels.

STAMEN The pollen-producing part of the plant.

SUCCULENT A thick-leaved plant such as a cactus that stores water in its stems and leaves.

SWIM BLADDER Part of the body of a fish which can be filled with air, and stops it from sinking.

THERMAL Hot air current which blows upwards.

THORAX The central part of an insect's body. The wings and legs are fixed to the thorax, which contains all the muscles that the insect uses to move them.

TUBER Swollen, usually underground stem or root, such as the potato.

TUNDRA Frozen treeless plain found close to the Arctic.

ULTRAVIOLET Colour or light with a short wavelength which the human eye cannot see. To insects, it is a pale shade of blue.

VERTEBRATE Animal with a bony skeleton and a backbone. Fish, amphibians, reptiles, birds, and mammals are all vertebrates.
See also MAMMAL, REPTILE.

ZOOPLANKTON Microscopic crustaceans, fish larvae, and other aquatic animals.

Index

A

abalone 78
abdomen 61–63, 71, 91
acacia 116
Acer pseudoplatanus 51
acontia 73
Actias selene 67
Actinia equina 146
actinopterygians 27
Aepyornis maximus 33
African clawed toad 81
African jaçana 137
African lungfish 26
African mud turtle 152
African spiny-tailed lizard 87
agave 118
air 76, 77, 80, 129, 154
air bladder 158
air pressure 66, 112, 151
air turbulence 151
Aix galericulata 88
albatross 32, 174, 175
albino 81
alder, common 141; cones 141
algae 115, 144, 146, 156, 165;
  chalky 162
alligator snapping turtle 152
Alnus glutinosa 141
Alocasia thibautiana 179
Alopex lagopus 128
alpine daphne 107
alpine meadow 108
Alps 113
altitude 106, 108, 151; low 110
altocumulus 102
altostratus 102
Amazonian water-lily 137
amber 11
Ambystoma mexicanus 81
Ambystoma tigrinum 80
ammonite 10
amniotes 28
amoeba 15
amphibians 10, 81–83, 140, 141, 177;
  ancestors 10, 28; swimming 82, 83;
  walking 82, 83
Amphiprion 164
anaconda 84
Anas crecca 138
anchovy 27
anemones 25, 70–73, 147
Anemonia sulcata 147
angelfish 27
angler fish 173
Angraecum sesquipedale 114
angwantibo 98
annelids 72
annual seablite 143
Antarctic 18, 21, 101, 110, 126, 127,
  160, 174; ice fish 128
anteater 35
antelope 54, 116
antennae 56, 57, 60–62, 66, 67, 141,
  155; dentate 67; pectinate 67
antennule 155
anther 39, 45–47
anthrax 14
anti-freeze 128
antlers 179
ant lion 120
ants 58, 87
Appias nero 56

B

Aptenodytes fosteri 126
Apteryx Australis 88
aquarium oxygenation 134
Aquila chrysaetos 89, 111
Aquilegia vulgaris 51
arboreal 124, 125
Archaeopteryx 32, 33
archer fish 140
Arctic 94, 95, 110, 150, 160, 179–181,
  183
Arctic fox 129, 129
aroid 179
arthropods 10
ash 105;
  volcanic 19, 20
asparagus, wild 42
Aster tripolium 142
atoll 163
Atolla 173
Australian bandicoot 181
Australian water-holding frog 81
Austropotamobius pallipes 141
axolotl 81
Aythya fuligula 139

backbones, fish 74
bacteria 14, 16, 38, 165, 170, 171;
  luminous 173; sulphur-fixing 170
baggy patch 80
baleen plates 168
baleen whale 168, 169
bamboo 108
bananas 166
barbels 133
bark 109, 116, 125
barnacle 70, 73
barometer 112, 113
barrel cactus 119
Baryonyx 31
basalt 20
bats 32, 44, 90, 91, 118, 140; fringed
  tongue 91
beadlet anemone 72, 73
beak 30, 32;
  bird 32; dinosaur 30
bean clams 68
bearded ark shell 154
bearded dragon 86, 87
beavers 92
bees 46, 47
beetles 55, 58, 59, 88, 98, 183;
  water 140
Belodon 29
bends, the 76
berries 50, 88, 128
Bhutan Glory 109
Bhutanitis lidderdalei 109
biological control (insects) 57
biosphere 16, 17
bird colonies 126, 127
birds 28, 32, 33, 44, 49, 50, 59, 60, 67,
  86, 88, 91, 98, 99, 101, 109–111, 115,
  117, 120–124, 126–129, 140, 148,
  149, 174, 175, 178, 180, 181, 183;
  flightless 88, 122, 12, 126, 127;
  heaviest 117; ringing 181;
  tallest 117
birth 96
birth rate 181
bivalves 68, 69, 78, 79, 154
black bean 53
black-browed albatross 174, 175
black coral 162
black crake 88
Black Death 93

C

black-necked stilt 148
black rhinoceros 116
bladder 81; air 158
bladder wrack 158
Blennius pholis 146
blenny 146, 156
blizzards 128
blood 76, 80, 90, 91, 117,
  126, 169, 179
blow-holes 95, 169
blubber 94, 127, 129, 174
bluebell 46, 47
bluebottles 61
blue mussels, common 154
blue-striped snapper 76
Blue-triangle butterfly 62
blue whale 12, 76, 168, 169
boa constrictor 84, 85
bombs and blocks 106
Bombycidae 64
Bombyx mori 64
bones 16, 21, 22, 24, 26–28, 30,
  32, 35, 84, 91, 172
bony crest 30, 32
bony frill 30
bony shield 26
boom or bust cycle 181
Borneo fruit bat 90
botanists 42
Botticelli, Sandro 68
Bouvier's crab 154
boxer crab 70
Brachypelma smithi 56
bract 39, 44, 48, 49
brain 26, 31, 91, 98
brain coral 163
branch 39, 42, 44, 96, 98, 99, 114,
  116, 123–125, 141, 144
breadcrumb sponge 147
breeding cycle 58, 88, 110, 174, 175
breeding season 90, 94, 101, 121,
  126, 127, 139, 153
breeze 49, 136, 150, 151; land 151;
  sea 151
brine shrimp 120
brittlestar 24, 146; fossil 24
broad bean 52
brocaded carp 133
brood patch 126, 127
brown kiwi 88
bubonic plague 93
buddleia 63
buds 39, 40, 46, 56, 51; flower 39;
  insect wing 59;
  lateral 39
bugs 58
bulb 41
bulbils 179, 182
bulbous rush 135
bumblebee 46
burrowing 56, 80–83, 86, 92, 93, 120,
  121, 129, 140, 152, 165
bushbaby 98, 99; greater 99;
  lesser 99
butterflies 12, 46, 47, 55, 56, 58,
  60–63, 66, 109, 115
butterfly blenny 157
butterfly fish 74
butterfly wings 68
buzzard 110
byssal threads 22, 69, 154

cacti 118, 119
caddis flies 58
caecilians 82, 83

caiman 84
Cairina moschata 139
Calamus caesius 115
calcium 34
calcium carbonate 16
California king snake 85
California newt 81
Caligo idomeneus 60, 61
calliactis anemone 70
Calliactis parasitica 70
Calliostoma zizphinum 146
camel 182
Canada lynx 108
Canadian waterweed 134
cane furniture 115
canopy 114, 115, 144;
  evergreen 114
capsule 39
caracal 120
carapace 155, 157
carbohydrate 16, 17
carbon 16, 17;
  inorganic 17; organic 17
carbon cycle 17
carbon dioxide 16, 17, 40, 119, 178
Carboniferous period 17
Carcharodon carcharias 77
caribou 179
carnivores 17, 28, 30, 31, 146
carnosaurs 31
carotenoids 12
carp 132, 133
carpel 44
carragheen 158, 159
cassowaries 123
caterpillars 55, 58, 60, 61,
  64–66, 98, 137
cat 94, 122
cat family 178
cattle 13, 105, 116
cave dwellers 81, 91, 94, 120
cells, single 14, 15
centipedes 55
century plant 118
cephalaspids 26
Cephalaspis pagei 26
cephalopods 78, 79
Ceratophyllum demersum 134
CFCs 178
Chaenocephalus aceratus 128
chambered nautilus 76
chameleon 86, 123
cheek pouches 92, 93
cheetah 85, 115
cheliped 70, 71, 141, 155, 165
chelonians 152, 153; hidden-necked
  152; marine 152; side-necked 152
chemosynthesis 170
chicks 110, 126, 127, 138,
  149, 174, 175
chill factor 108
chimneys, underwater 170, 171
china mark moth 137
chinchillas 92
Chinese soft-shelled turtle 140
chipmunk 17, 92
Chiroxiphia caudata 178
chlorophyll 12, 15, 40, 41, 158
chloroplasts 40, 41
chrysalis, *see* pupa
chrysanthemum shells 68
Chrysolophus Amherstiae 108
cilia 15, 72
cirrocumulus 102, 103
cirrostratus 102, 103
cirrus 102, 103
Cirsium arvense 51
cistanche plant 119
cladodes 42

clams 68, 69, 78
clasper 77
claws 31–33, 35, 87, 88, 90, 91, 93, 95, 115, 122, 123, 125, 129, 144, 145, 165, 180
clay 35
clematis 44, 45
climate 12, 20, 23, 106, 112, 131, 150, 151; fluctuations in 20, 177; mountain 108, 109; prehistoric 21
Clossiana euphrosyne 62
clothes moth 66
cloud cover 112, 151
cloud of ink 78, 79
clouds 102, 103, 112, 113, 150, 151, 167; feeder 113; summit 113
cloven hoof 116
clown anemone 164
clown fish 164; tomato 71
coachwhip plant 118
coal 17, 178
coastal weather 150, 151
coats 126, 179
cobra 121
cockchafer beetle 57
cockle 143
cockroach 58, 120
cock's-comb oyster 69
coconut 122; crab 122
cocoon 64, 80, 81
cod 74, 183
coelacanth 27, 182; fossil 27
coelenterates 70, 72, 73
cold front 113
coleoptile 52
Coleridge, Samuel 174
collared lizard 87
colonies 148
colour camouflage 62, 65, 74, 75, 78, 79, 86, 88, 89, 95, 119, 123, 128, 129, 132, 133, 135, 139, 144, 155–157, 164, 165, 179, 180; summer 128, 129; winter 180
coloured rings 103
columbine 51
comet orchid 114
Compsognathus 32
conches 147
concretion 26
cone shells 147
conger eels 75
conifer forests 108
conifers 30, 51; cones 51, 105, 108
conservation 181
conserving energy 126
continental drift 25
continental shelf 160, 161
continental slope 160, 161
copper 170
coral 10, 25, 72, 73, 157, 160–164; caves 164, 165; fossilized 25; meat-eating 164
coral reefs 27, 73, 75, 122, 162–165
coral snake 182
cord grass 143
corolla 66
Corythosaurus 30
cotyledon 39, 52, 53
couch grass 142
countershading 132
courtship display 82, 101, 149, 175
cowries 147
crab larva 12
crabs 25, 70, 71, 79, 122, 123, 130, 143–146, 154, 155, 165; shore 70, 71, 155
cranium 99

creeping thistle 51
crinoid 25
crocodile 31
crop destruction 66, 90
crop, flamingo's 148
crops 181
crustaceans 25, 68–71, 74, 79, 140, 141, 146, 147, 154, 155, 161, 183; desert 120; giant 122
crustal plate 170
cumulonimbus 102, 103, 167
cumulus 102, 103, 150
cup coral 73
cushion star 146
cuttlefish 78
cyclone 166
Cyclorana platycephalus 81
Cygnus olor 13

D

dab 156
Dacelo novaeguineae 124
daisies 44
dandelion 48, 49
dark zone 172
Darwin, Charles 66, 163
Darwin's hawkmoth 66
date palm 118
dates 118
death rate 181
decomposers 16
decomposition 17, 22, 23, 34, 35, 180
deer 84
defence 35, 141, 144, 152, 175
dehydration 52, 115, 144
deltas 20
Deltavjatia vjatkensis 29
Dendrolagus dorianus 125
depressions 150
desert fox 120
desert hedgehog 120, 121
desert nomads 118
deserts 17, 80, 81, 86, 87, 92, 93, 101, 116, 118–121, 182; Australia 86, 87; Jordan 119; Kalahari 119; Namib 86, 118, 119, 121; Sahara 86, 87; USA 118
desmids 15
dew 118–120
diapause 60
diatom 14, 15
dicotyledons 38, 39, 53
digestion 84, 85
digestive system 62, 72, 73
Dimetrodon 28
dinosaurs 11, 25, 27, 28, 30–32, 35, 168; bird-hipped 30, 31; reptile-hipped 30, 31
Diplazium proliferum 179
Diplomystus dentatus 27
diseases 66, 182; in cattle 66
disguises 156, 157
dog 91
dogfish 12
dog rose 44, 45
dolphins 12, 76, 77, 126, 161, 179
Doria's tree kangaroo 125
down 126, 174
drag (water resistance) 76, 79
dragonflies 32, 56, 58, 140
drift nets 179
drip tip 115
droppings 50, 90
drought 118
duck 30, 134, 138, 139, 148
dulse 158, 159

dunlin 148
dye 115
Dyscophis antongili 114

E

eagle 110, 111
early flying machine 174
ears 91, 93, 94, 98, 99, 125, 129; flaps 93; tufts 120
earthquakes 18, 20
earth's crust 161, 170
earthworms 72
echidna 34
echo-location 90, 91
ecologists 181
ecosystem 17, 90
Edaphosaurus 28
edible crab 157
edible periwinkle 147
eel 132, 172
eggs 17, 23, 30, 31, 33, 55, 57–61, 64, 66, 71, 81, 86–88, 110, 117, 120, 121, 125–127, 137, 149, 152, 153, 162, 164, 183; case 143; colour 60; hatching 55, 60, 64, 87, 120, 127, 133; insect 57, 60, 61; largest 117; laying 30, 31, 34, 55, 117; silkworm 64
eiderdown 138
eider duck 138
electric ray 76, 77
electron micrograph 15
Eledone cirrhosa 79
elephant 16, 168, 176; African 176; bull 168
elephant bird 33
Elodea canadensis 134
elytra 57
embryo 52
emergents 114
Emperor moth 67
Emperor penguin 126, 127
encrusting anemone 73
endangered species 63, 114, 169
endemism 177
endosperm 52
energy 35, 40, 41, 146, 167, 182; chemical 40; light 41
epaulette shark 77
epidermis 44
Epilachna varivestis 58
equator 126
Equus burchelli 117
Erigeron borealis 182
erosion 21, 22, 154
estuary 142–144, 148, 158
eucalyptus 42
eucalyptus gum tree 124
European crayfish 141
European eel 172
European fire salamander 82, 83
European John Dory 74
Eupharynx pelecanoides 172
evaporation 142, 160
exoskeleton 56, 140, 141, 165
extinction 30, 31, 178, 182
eyed lizard 87
eyeless shrimp 170
eyes 25–27, 29, 31, 66, 67, 78, 79, 90, 93, 98, 99, 110, 111, 114, 125, 145, 155–157, 165, 172–174, 183; binocular-like 173; compound 56, 62; fish 74, 76; simple 59, 60; sockets 99
eye of storm 166, 167

eye wall 166
eyespots 67, 109, 164
eyrie 89

F

falcon 110, 111
Falco rusticolus 111
family group 54, 100
fault line 20
fan worm 72
feather star 25
feathers 20, 32, 33, 88, 89, 108, 110, 126–129, 138, 139, 175, 180; fossilized 20, 33; primary flight 89, 139; tail 108
feeding 24–26, 62, 66, 70–75, 77, 81, 90–95, 114, 115, 161, 164, 165
feet 62, 78, 81–83, 88, 95, 124–128, 175; webbing on 81, 82, 86, 87, 138, 144, 174
femur 24
ferns 28, 179
fertilization 46, 53
Ficus religiosa 115
fiddler crab 144, 145
fig leaf 115
filament 39, 45
filter feeding 149, 168
fingers 32, 91, 96, 98
fin ray 173
fins 26, 27, 74–77, 132, 133, 165, 168, 172
fire fountain 106
fire thorn 118
fish 26, 27, 31, 108, 124, 126, 127, 130, 132, 133, 135, 139–141, 146, 149, 164, 165, 170, 172–174, 181, 182; advanced bony 26, 27; ancient 26, 27; deep-sea 172, 173; freshwater 132, 133, 135; jawless 26; lobe-finned 27; ray-finned 27
fish-eater 32
fishing 179
fish traps 115
flamingoes 148, 149
flatfish 156, 157
fleas 58, 93
Flexicalymene caractaci 21
flies 91, 140
flight 32, 33, 37, 46, 47, 56, 57, 60, 63, 66, 67, 88–91, 110, 139, 140, 148; first 32, 33
flipper 24, 25, 126, 153
flood plains 20
florets 44, 45, 48; disc 44; ray 44
flower 20, 38, 39, 41, 44–51, 53, 62, 66–68, 72, 104, 105, 116, 118, 134, 136, 137, 142, 183; alpine 109, 113; composite 44, 45, 48; floating 136, 137; fossil 20; shape 44–47; simple 44, 45
fluted giant clam 69
flying fish 76
flying fox 90, 91
flying lemur 91
flying squirrel 91
fog 150; advection 150; coastal 150
food 17, 30–32, 34, 35, 38, 39, 54, 55, 57, 68, 72, 73, 78, 80, 88–91, 94, 95, 108, 120–125, 128, 1129, 132–134, 138–141, 146–149, 154, 162, 168, 170–175, 180–183; for plants 12, 38–41, 46; storage 92–94, 105, 128
footprint 20; fossilized 20

Acknowledgments

Dorling Kindersley would like to thank

Susila Baybars and Marion Dent for editorial
assistance; Ivan Finnegan, Cormac Jordan,
Sailesh Patel, and Susan St Louis for design
assistance; and Alex Arthur, David Burnie,
David Carter, Jack Challoner, Dr Barry Clarke,
Brian Cosgrove, John Farndon, Theresa
Greenaway, William Lindsay, Dr Miranda
MacQuitty, Colin McCarthy, Laurence Mound,
Vassili Papastavrou, Steve Parker, Steve Pollock,
Ian Redmond, Scott Steadman, Barbara Taylor,
Dr Paul D. Taylor, Susanna van Rose and
Paul Whalley for contributing to the book

Special Photography
Peter Anderson, Geoff Brightling, Jane Burton,
Peter Chadwick, Andy Crawford, Geoff Dann,
Philip Dowell, John Downes, Neil Fletcher,
Steve Gorton, Frank Greenaway, Colin Keates,
Dave King, Cyril Laubscher, Mike Linley,
Andrew McRobb, Karl Shone, James Stevenson,
Clive Streeter, Harold Taylor, Kim Taylor,
Andreas von Einsiedel, Spike Walker,
Jerry Young

Illustrators
Simone End, Andrew Macdonald, Richard Orr,
Sallie Alane Reason, Colin Salmon,
Richard Ward, John Woodcock, Dan Wright

Model makers
David Donkin, John Downes, Peter Griffiths,
Graham High and Jeremy Hunt/Centaur
Studios, John Holmes

Index
Marion Dent

Picture research
Lorna Ainger, Katie Bradshaw, Liz Cooney,
John Stevenson